WILLIAM JUBB

From Promise to Disaster

Darling Downs 1845-1878

BRIAN HANSFORD

Copyright © Brian Hansford 2018

All rights reserved. No part of this book may be reproduced by any means, except where permitted under the Copyright Act, without the written permission of the publisher.

Inspire Point Publishing
PO Box 972
Beenleigh, Queensland 4207
Australia
Email: admin@inspirepointpublishing.com

 A catalogue record for this book is available from the National Library of Australia

Designed by Peta Hansford

William Jubb: From Promise to Disaster, Darling Downs 1845-1878
ISBN: 978-0-6482981-0-6

Table of Contents

Acknowledgments	v
Illustrations & Copyright Permission	ix
Introduction	3
The Beginnings	6
Jubb and Joseph Gordon	9
Jubb at Shepherd's Crossing	12
Jubb as a Builder	16
Goomburra Run	20
Glennie at Jubbs	22
Leslie Mentions Jubbs	24
Remains of Jubb's Inn	26
Blacksmith's Requirements	28
Jubb 'A Jack of All Trades'	30
Alphen at Woolpack Inn	33
Sociocultural Considerations	35
Jubb Acquires the Woolpack Inn	38
Jubb's Religious Affiliations	41
Perceptions of the Jubbs	42

Arnold Wienholt	46
Margaret Jubb	48
Horses Stolen and Wallet Lost	51
Trips to Sydney	53
Shambles at Parramatta	55
Other Business	59
Servants at the Woolpack	61
Jubb Brothers and Alcohol	64
Jubb's Bank Account	69
George Jubb	78
Shipping Intelligence	82
Woolpack Inn Ownership	85
Cattle Stealing	90
David Robinson	94
Where Did William Jubb Go?	97
Jubb at Wolston Park	99
Jubb's Death	102
Eleanor Jubb	104
Reflecting on Jubb	106
Postscript – Jubbs (Tubbs) Were Farmers	116
William Jubb Timeline	119
Endnotes	123
Sources	127
Index of People	131

Acknowledgments

While completing *The Elusive Archibald Young* (2016) it was frequently noted references were made to a man called William Jubb the innkeeper at Woolpack Inn near Cunninghams Gap. These notations seemed to suggest that Jubb was an interesting personality in the Darling Downs District. The decision to follow the William Jubb paper trail has been quite demanding, surprising, sad and at times even alarming.

As this book commenced it was thought that it would be the story of an innkeeper. True, Jubb spent much of his time as an innkeeper at the Woolpack Inn, but that is only half the story. One historian described Jubb as a 'jack of all trades' and this expression seems to provide a more comprehensive and accurate perspective of the life of Jubb.

Actually knowing virtually nothing about Jubb it was surprising to find information about him being at Dalrymple Creek (Allora) prior to taking over the Woolpack Inn. Some serious 'Jubb followers' associated with the Allora Historical Society Inc. were located. Initial contact was made with Colin Newport who had written a couple of articles in the *Allora Advertiser* about Jubb and the building he had constructed on the edge of Dalrymple Creek. Colin's associate Trevor Neale had also spent considerable time searching for information about Jubb. I would like to personally thank Colin and Trevor. Without the enthusiasm of such people the early history of local areas will remain hidden or simply disappear. During the writing of this book Colin has received enough queries from me to choke an elephant. Thank you for your tolerance.

This publication was initially to be dedicated to the memory of William Jubb, but as the story developed, it was felt his brother George Jubb warranted a special mention in the dedication. The Jubbs were not the 'great' historic figures we heard about at school such as John Macarthur, Governor Bligh, Ned Kelly or Captain Cook. They represented the thousands of small cogs who got in and did something to help make our convict dominated communities into a real country.

As in previous writing adventures I have ranted and raved about copyright regulations and digitised newspapers not providing the answers I required. My wife Jean has easily coped with these outbursts over many years. I would like to simply thank Jean for her love and understanding. Jean also acted as a volunteer research assistant at the State Library of Queensland.

This account draws heavily upon the digitised newspapers contained within *Trove*. In the consideration of the life of Jubb these newspapers provide the data for a major part of his story. Jan Ward-Brown's book *Rosenthal-Historic Shire* (1988) of 788 pages examined primary sources that are not easily accessed. Unfortunately, this informative publication does not provide a detailed name and location index, making the cross-checking of information difficult. This historian accessed such records as those of Rolleston the Crown Land Commissioner, various relevant diaries and record books of stations including Maryland Run. Such sources provided information regarding Jubb.

Thank you to Queensland State Archives, State Library of Queensland, Althea Vickers of North Stradbroke Historical Museum, professional genealogist Judy Webster, Dr Barry Hall for editing assistance and Stephen Kerwin who I 'bugged' about photographs and then changed my mind. Lisa Hopkinson (Westpac Group Archive) and Peter Marinick (ANZ Group Archive) were extremely helpful in their endeavours to locate the financial records of William Jubb. Jo Pollard, graphic designer at the Samford Typing and Copy Centre was an excellent resource person when my computer failed to carry out shouted commands. Des Byrne was again a great sounding board for all types of queries regarding reproducing documents and issues relating to publication. In general, members of the Samford 'Thursday lunch think tank' were more interested in their longevity, superannuation balances, upcoming medical and cruise arrangements than my concerns relating to the life of William Jubb.

Peta Hansford of Inspire Point Publishing was extremely generous with her assistance relating to cover design, placement of illustrations and publication issues generally.

Illustrations & Copyright Permission

These numbered illustrations appear in this publication:

1. Mud Map – 'Jubb's Area' in the Southern Downs
2. Allora Survey by George Pratten, (1859)
3. Painting of Mrs Jubb's Public House, (Montagu 1853)
4. Rose and Crown Hotel Parramatta, (1870–1890)
5. Signatures Extracted from Cheques and Supreme Court Writ, (Cheques June 1858 and Affidavit March 1859)
6. Summary Jubb's Bank Account, (1856–1858)
7. Map of Woolpack Inn Sale Site, (1859)

Copyright Permissions

i. *Allora Survey 1859 by George Pratten.* Permission no longer required, 2017.

ii. *Mrs Jubbs Public House (Montagu 1853).* Permission granted to use Item PID Negative Number 202300 by State Library of Queensland, 2017.

iii. *Black and white photograph of Rose and Crown Hotel circa, 1870s–1890s.* Permission granted to use object LSP00700 by Heritage Centre Photographic Collection, City of Parramatta, 2017.

iv. *Survey Plans A.1708.1 (Sheets 1-10) and Mt.54.* Permission granted for use by the Department of Natural Resources and Mines, 2017.

v. *QSA ID 2320431 Jubb v Fleming (1859) Supreme Court Writ.* Discussion between Queensland State Archives and the Brisbane Supreme Court decided 'that in this case copyright does not exist. Therefore no permission to reproduce this item is needed', 2017.

vi. *ANZ Group Archive Victoria.* No copyright required but approval granted for reproduction in book, 2017.

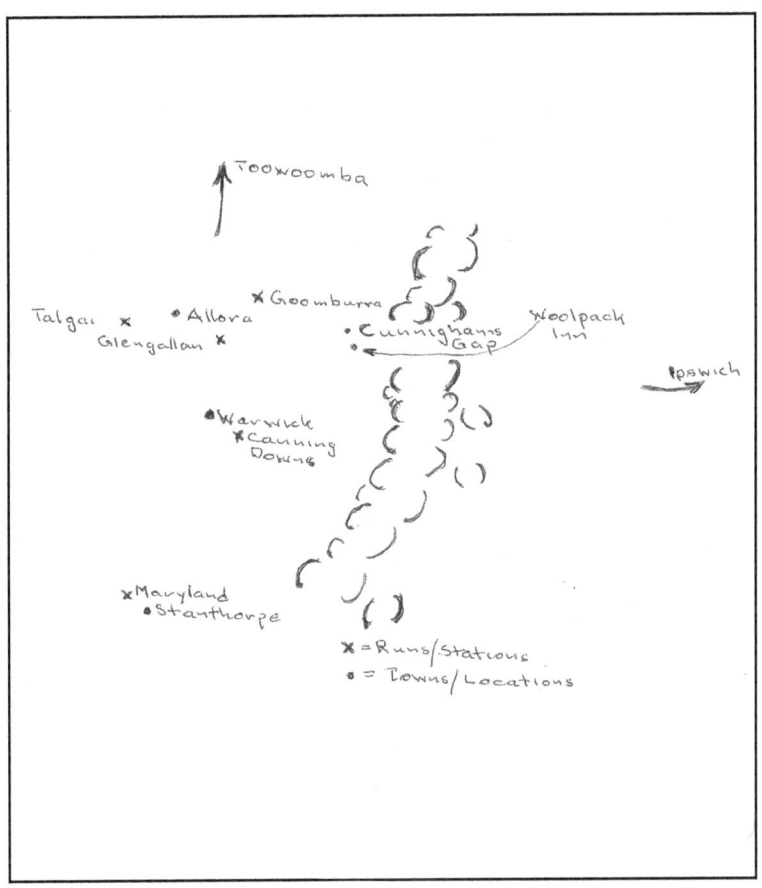

1. Mud Map – 'Jubb's Area' in the Southern Downs

Introduction

The early publicans and innkeepers of colonial Australia provided a service to a small, and in many instances, rather mobile population. Mobile, because a considerable proportion of the population was seeking improved opportunities and a better life than they had previously experienced.

Initially, there was a clear distinction between an innkeeper and a publican. An innkeeper was responsible for a business that sold alcohol but also provided accommodation for travellers, stables for horses and in the more remote areas holding yards or paddocks for stock. Publicans were in charge of businesses where alcohol was sold and these were generally described as public houses, normally located in towns. The differences between inns and public houses and innkeepers and publicans became blurred when public houses commenced providing meals and stables for horses.

The majority of people in colonial Australia were endeavouring to make their way in an unfamiliar land viewed by many of the new arrivals as harsh and dangerous. As the profits of publicans were linked to the sales of alcohol, the watering down of products benefited financial reserves as did access to illicit stills. There were of course those who did not officially become publicans or innkeepers, that is, they did not seek a liquor licence. These were the sly groggers who practised their skills from secluded bush lean-tos or tents and used swift packhorses or light well sprung drays to ensure maximum mobility for relocation.

Prior to 1850, the *Moreton Bay Courier* reported a number of sly groggers operating in the region. For example, in 1847 William Crabb, a stable keeper in South Brisbane, had his ticket-of-leave cancelled for operating 'a disorderly sort of house where illicit drinking was encouraged'. In 1849 Joseph Sedolla was fined £100 for running an illicit still in New Farm. At Warwick, in 1848, bullock drivers named Hold and Gilbert 'bolted' following a charge of selling illegal grog. Timothy Shea the well-known 'travelling shepherd' or 'flying shepherd' was charged in May 1849 with dealing in illicit grog. He argued that the noble rural occupation of shepherd practised by himself and his forefathers was no longer profitable enough and that he would need to again subsidise his income in the future. In the previous month, April 1849, Shea had been apprehended for an Ipswich warrant and placed on the Arora anchored in the Mary River, he escaped and swam ashore.

Those involved in sly grog avoided social contact with the precursors to real estate salesmen, building inspectors, insurance agents, parking officers, tax collectors and the constabulary who strove to enforce the law.

It should be kept in mind that a number of these isolated inns became the meeting place for men and women who had left their old worlds behind them. In many ways it was irrelevant whether a person's origin was convict or free settler, as many became lonely, frustrated and depressed; the inn offered the possibility of human contact.

Although the officials of the colony of New South Wales (NSW) were quick to introduce liquor licensing this did not avoid a serious problem arising from the sale of alcohol in an environment largely built upon a citizenry of convict origin. Surprisingly little has been written about the personalities who became licensed publicans in remote locations. An exception to this would be Judith Grimes's (2013) account of Jacob Goode in *Jacob Goode and his Burnett Inn*. Goode, a larger than life figure, started at Brisbane and moved on to Nanango where the historic Burnett Inn was established. However, Grimes pointed out that ten years of excessive drinking caused his death and the demise of his dreams.

This book also considers the frequently complex and rather turbulent life of William Jubb who joined what might be rather loosely described as the hospitality industry in the colony of NSW during the early 1840s to 1859. It also contains information regarding several of the somewhat different members of the extended Jubb family.

The Beginnings

It has proved difficult to provide a convincing story regarding Jubb who was born in Ireland and later arrived in NSW. There were convicts and free settlers who arrived in the colony named William Jubb. However, to make a defensible connection to a William Jubb who spent much of the 1840s and 1850s in the Darling Downs District was another matter. Jubb had a brother named George who, just to make things more complex, was born in NSW. The parents of the Jubb boys, well at least the mother, apparently moved to NSW in the period between the two births. By working backwards from William Jubb's death certificate you can ascertain that he was born in 1813 and died in 1878. Based on George Jubb's death certificate of 1896 he was born in NSW in 1821. The use of death certificates to establish potential birth dates in the 1800s is clearly not the ideal situation. During much of the 1850s, Jubb was an innkeeper near Cunninghams Gap at the Woolpack Inn on Gap Creek. For part of the 1840s he was involved in a not unrelated activity at Dalrymple Creek (Allora). Although the literature tends to refer to Jubb as an innkeeper he was also a blacksmith, as was his brother George.

William Jubb: From Promise to Disaster 7

There were many personalities like William Jubb in the early years of the Australian colonies, but unlike the squattocracy and senior public officials, little is known about them. They just disappear from our history. Most did not keep diaries and they rarely wrote letters to significant colonial figures or members of society in their home countries. Their lives were focused on survival and, if they did write letters to relatives or friends such communications have long since disappeared. The early newspapers do contain some notations regarding publicans and the like, but these often occurred when people like innkeepers were involved in breeches of the law or acted in a manner which upset members of the upper echelons of society.

There was also the problem that a number of these early Australians were illiterate. The *Brisbane Courier,* in May 1892, carried an article about how the then State of Queensland had grown since a census in 1846. In 1846 the County of Stanley, which included the towns of Brisbane and Ipswich had 1599 people and the Darling Downs 659. In excess of 50% of the adult population in Stanley County could neither read nor write.[1]

It is likely that those living on the Darling Downs at this time would have similar reading and writing problems. It will be shown later in this account that some believed Jubb to be an illiterate. However, it also seems likely that his writing ability was influenced by the state of his health.

When deciding to write about Jubb there was awareness that it would be difficult to obtain complete information about his entire life. The hope was that sufficient information would be obtained to provide a comprehensive account of who this man was and what he did in the colony.

Jubb and Joseph Gordon

In May 1845 there was a reference to Jubb in the documents of Christopher Rolleston, the then Commissioner for Crown Lands, Darling Downs. Rolleston's records indicate Jubb and Thomas Lynch gave evidence against Joseph Gordon who had been charged with larceny, forgery and uttering. Gordon was a convict who in 1835 arrived in the colony of NSW. We may tend to think that most of the convicts arriving in NSW were transported for trivial offences by harsh and unjust laws. In part this is correct, but a diverse range of individuals arrived in the colonies from murderers to those who probably committed no real offence. These exiles formed the base of the initial Australian labour force. Gordon was one of those rather different convicts.

It is not clear what evidence Jubb and Lynch gave concerning Gordon, but in mid-1845 Jubb was most likely employed on the Goomburra Run by the Aberdeen Company. It is uncertain where Lynch worked, perhaps it was with Jubb. The *Moreton Bay Courier* does report the death of a Thomas Lynch in June 1847. During a trip from Brisbane to Coopers Plains he ran away into the bush and was later found dead holding his prayer book.

On 30 May 1845 Rolleston placed a £10 reward notice in the government gazette. The reward was for the capture of Gordon who had escaped from the Border Police Station, Darling Downs.[2]

The *Gazette* notice indicated that Gordon faced 'divers charges of fraud, forgery and other misdemeanours'. His trade in the United Kingdom was given as 'chymist and druggist'. He had also been 'a shoe maker and had served in the Royal Artillery'. In the general remarks, the notice claimed that 'he was of plausible speech, quick delivery and adept at forgery'.

A few months later Gordon was arrested in Sydney. The *Examiner*, on 18 October 1845, reported that Gordon had been before the Supreme Court, Darlinghurst and found guilty of forgery and uttering.[3]

The person he attempted to defraud was Thomas Alford, a pioneer on the Darling Downs at Drayton and Toowoomba. A few days later the *Australian*, on 21 October 1845, claimed that Gordon 'had been carrying on a course of most imprudent deceptions and forgeries'.[4]

His sentence was that he should be transported for ten years. No, he was not sent back to the UK. It is possible that he was sent to another penal colony although a number of repeat offenders or recidivists, such as Gordon, were sent to Norfolk Island. This was a penal colony referred to as 'hell in the Pacific'.

Many of the people Jubb knew or lived among were exiles from their native countries. A number of these were illiterate. Some were skilled conmen like Gordon and a number were the dregs of the UK population. For the thousands, like Jubb, who were eking out a living in unfamiliar surroundings and among a rather peculiar population just surviving was an extreme challenge.

Jubb at Shepherd's Crossing

In the early 1840s a few shepherds established huts on the Warwick-Drayton road where it crossed Dalrymple Creek. This became known as Shepherd's Crossing and it was an excellent stopping place for teamsters bringing supplies for runs such as Glengallan and Talgai. However, the promise of the Darling Downs also ensured stockmen, labourers, timber-getters and those opportunists or adventurers seeking a new and better life also stopped over.

In 1902 the *Toowoomba Chronicle and Darling Downs General Advertiser* reported a story that was also in other local newspapers regarding the recollections of Edward Anderson, a Darling Downs pioneer. He suggested that on his first visit to the Shepherd's Crossing on Dalrymple Creek in 1844 the only house there was that of Neil Ross and his wife from Scotland. Ross had been employed by the Leslies as a stockman but later became a successful land owner in his own right. Samuel Gordon from Northern Ireland and Jacob Bleaker from Germany were other early occupiers of huts near Dalrymple Creek and both were shepherds for the Leslies.[5]

Anderson actually replaced Jubb at Goomburra as blacksmith and builder although he worked for Patrick Leslie, the then occupant of the run.

Jubb was at the Dalrymple Creek crossing before 1846 as in that year he twice applied for a building licence from Rolleston. At that time Jubb was described as a blacksmith from Goomburra. Jan Ward-Brown (1988) in her chapter on Goomburra Run in *Rosenthal Historic Shire* reports that Jubb worked for the Aberdeen Company (North British Australian Company) as a blacksmith and wheelwright. He was more than this, and Ward-Brown points out that for a period of time 'Jubb was the only licensed builder in the Warwick District'. It was the general policy for the Aberdeen Company to import Scottish employees and thus Jubb, an Irishman, may have been somewhat of an outsider at this work location. Based on comments regarding licensed builders by Ward-Brown, it would seem that Jubb held such a licence from 1845 to perhaps 1849. Later in this book evidence is provided that Jubb maintained an association with building and builders well into his time at Woolpack Inn.

The record book of Rolleston for 1851 indicates that two exiles, James Bolton and James Horton, had been assigned to a person described as the 'Warwick Carpenter'. Ward-Brown suggests this carpenter may well have been Jubb. However, she also raises the possibility that Rolleston, who liked things to be 'neat', may have assigned the two exiles to themselves, a practice he had used previously.

In the book *Rosenthal* the author draws attention to the fact that for some period of time after Jubb left the Aberdeen Company he continued to use money orders drawn on John Taylor manager of the Aberdeen Company to pay his licence fee. The Aberdeen Company purchased Goomburra from Ernest Dalrymple for £300 and, as these were depression years, the company may have released Jubb from his work agreement thus decreasing their ongoing expenses. Whether the link to Taylor was in some way related to his severance conditions from the company or even a reflection of Jubb's poor literacy skills is a matter for conjecture.[6]

In the next section there is a closer examination of Jubb as a builder and his link to John Taylor. This is largely based on the transcription of Land Commissioner Rolleston's records by the Toowoomba and Darling Downs Family History Society Inc. (2008).

Jubb certainly had the building skills to construct the 'inn' on Dalrymple Creek. This establishment was a supply and blacksmith shop, and Jubb was joined there by his brother George, also a blacksmith. It is not known when the word 'inn' was attached to Jubb's building and it is possible that some type of accommodation was available during periods of heavy rain and flooding. There was however no licence to sell alcohol. A rumour has existed for some time that a chance event was responsible for Jubb settling at the creek. The unsubstantiated story is that Jubb arrived at the crossing during a period of heavy rain. His wagon became bogged and he decided this was the place he would set up at.

Torrential summer storms ensured that Dalrymple Creek could flood rapidly, causing delays of days for those wishing to cross the creek. Today we talk about 'location, location' for the establishing of a business, and the Dalrymple Crossing was a good location for a business concerned with the sale of supplies and repairs by a blacksmith. The waiting travellers would get hungry and thirsty and Jubb may also have provided food and other general supplies at the crossing. If alcohol was available it would have been welcomed by many of the travellers. Actually, Jubb and other embryonic businesses at the site probably prayed for torrential rain.

Jubb as a Builder

The hand written records of Commissioner Rolleston are a challenge, and the belated discovery of the 2008 transcription of his letters and records was an immense relief. This transcription seems to suggest some differences to those raised by Ward-Brown relating to Jubb.

One of the major tasks for Rolleston was the issuing of various licences. As early as 1844 he wrote to the Colonial Secretary asking 'whether I am in charge of building licences'. Despite this concern and a lack of an appropriate building licence form he granted Thomas Alford a home and business premises building licence (Downs Inn) in 1844 at 'The Springs' (Drayton).

On 7 January 1846 Rolleston notified the Colonial Secretary that he had granted Jubb a building licence for six months and received the half year fee of £5. This fee was paid by an order on Henry Ferris, York St, Sydney. (Ferris was a commission agent who advertised in Sydney papers what he called 'Settlers Wholesale Current Prices'). Rolleston mentioned that the regulations regarding limits of settlement might change before the six months had elapsed. Rolleston again contacted the Colonial Secretary regarding Jubb on the 17 August, 1846. He had issued a year-long building licence to 'William Jubb, Blacksmith for Goomburra Creek'. This licence commenced on 1 July 1846.

Rolleston forwarded the Colonial Secretary a £10 building licence fee from William Jubb on 16 March 1848. This fee was covered by various money orders. One was a £2 10 - order signed by Taylor, that is John Taylor, of the Aberdeen Company. Roughly two months later, Rolleston on 22 May 1848 informed the Colonial Secretary that the £2 10 - order upon Mr John Taylor had been returned dishonoured. That did not complete the dealings with Jubb, and on the 15 August, 1848 Rolleston reported that 'the sum of Ten Pounds paid into my hands by William Jubb Blacksmith'. The 1848 licence had not turned up by 6 October 1848 and Rolleston again wrote saying 'the licence may be forwarded to my office when ready'.

When Rolleston completed his yearly returns for 1847/1848 and 1848/1849 William Jubb was listed as 'a person recommended for a building licence'.

Ward-Brown reported that John Taylor paid licence fees for Jubb after he ceased working for the Abdereen Company. One such instance of this was located in the Rolleston records for 1848, but the money order was dishonoured. It is possible that Ward-Brown had access to other records indicating additional involvements by Taylor. Given Taylor's access to resources and standing in the region, it is difficult to understand the dishonouring that did occur.

There is no doubt that Jubb held a building licence from at least 1846 to 1849, but where was he doing this work? It is highly likely that the 'inn' on Dalrymple Creek was completed in 1846. Several possibilities exist. Perhaps he still carried out work on the Goomburra Run or built houses for new arrivals in the local area. There were buildings approved at Drayton in 1846, 1848 and 1849, and Ward-Brown suggested he may have been involved in the construction of the Woolpack Inn, where it is noted that Alphen had a building licence for 1848 and 1849. A major query that arises is whether Jubb would travel as far as Gap Creek or Drayton to work when he was endeavouring to establish a blacksmith business on Dalrymple Creek.

Rolleston recommended building licences for the year ending 30 June 1848. These licences were:

Drayton: Thomas Alford (Storekeeper), William Handcock (Storekeeper), Peter Flanagan (Blacksmith), William Horton (Innkeeper), Stephen Mehan (Innkeeper), Henry Wilks (Surgeon), Thomas Gates (Carpenter)

Clifton: Charles Miles (Surgeon)

Goomburra: William Jubb (Blacksmith)

Gap Creek: Henry Alphen (Innkeeper)

The above 10 licences were for the construction of buildings where a commercial practice would be operated. The question as to who were the builders for these recommended structures is another matter. Jubb held a building licence for a period of years in the 1840s. Ward-Brown claimed that for some time Jubb was 'the only licensed builder in the Warwick district'. What and where was he building? Has some confusion occurred in terminology? Rolleston recommended building licenses rather than builder's licenses. It is known that Jubb built a blacksmith shop on Dalrymple Creek, but where were his other building activities?

Hall, in the *Early History of Warwick District*, named nine of the original carpenters and builders in the area. Jubb is not one of those named. This seems to be additional evidence of a confusion relating to builders or buildings in the Rosenthal text.

Goomburra Run

Goomburra was a prime stock run on the Southern Downs first occupied by Ernest Dalrymple in 1840, then the Aberdeen Company, and then Patrick Leslie. Goomburra had many of the characteristics of a small village and along with several neighbouring runs had social and political influence. As late as December 1861 when Mort and Company advertised Goomburra for sale in the *Empire* an impression was given of what existed at this run.[7]

The run was described as a magnificent sheep property, 12 to 13 miles from Warwick and adjacent to Canning Downs, Clifton, Talgai and Glengallan. The carrying capacity of the 45,000 acre run was 26,000 sheep and 800 head of cattle.

Improvements included a family residence with extensive vineyards and gardens. There was a woolshed, numerous stores and storekeeper's quarters. The property had accommodation (huts) for bachelors and other men, a blacksmith shop, and considerable stabling for horses. There were two paddocks under oats and lucerne and three large grazing paddocks with pure water. To this must be added horses, drays, working bullock teams, tools and equipment.

The blacksmith shop, mentioned in the Mort and Co 1861 advertisement, was certainly a place where Jubb worked, but it is not known when Jubb commenced work at the site. He certainly was there during part of the time when John Taylor was manager of the Aberdeen Company.

Glennie at Jubbs

There are a number of comments in early newspapers regarding Jubb but unfortunately the brevity of such statements often clouds their meaning. Benjamin Glennie, an Anglican minister, on the Darling Downs visited Jubbs at the Dalrymple Creek crossing in September 1848. At that time he was on his way to Goomburra. At Goomburra Glennie held a church service for 12 participants. *The Australian Diary of the Reverend Benjamin Glennie* is written in what might be described as summary or note form. 'Jubb's Goomburra' is again mentioned in a diary entry for September 1849 and may well have been associated with a baptism. There is another entry mentioning 'Jubbs' in May 1852. There had been heavy rain and waterways were rising. Glennie wrote that he had managed 'crossing Dalrymple Creek at Jubbs'. The diary indicates quite a number of days when Glennie visited Goomburra.

The *Moreton Bay Courier* reported that in 1848 Goomburra Run was approximately 45,000 acres and had the capacity to carry 10,000 sheep and 300 cattle. It should be noted that the number of stock which could be carried on the run had increased substantially by the time Mort and Company offered the run for sale in late 1861. A number of other well-known runs such as Canning Downs, Talgai, and Glengallen were also visited by Glennie. Inns such as 'Alphens' (Gap Creek), 'Perrymans' (Bush Inn at Fassifern) and 'John Collins large room' at Warwick were also noted in the diary. A number of sources claim that 'John Collins large room' was the Horse and Jockey Hotel at Warwick. This is disputed in the book *Rosenthal* where it is argued that the first church service in the Warwick area was held in

> the hall at Canning Downs and not in the Horse and Jockey Hotel as historians have claimed, which hotel had not been erected in August 1848.[8]

Despite recurring ill health, serious fatigue, and church financial problems, Glennie travelled thousands of miles on horse and on foot to ensure his message was delivered to those in lonely and frequently isolated locations. Some degree of understanding regarding the preaching of Glennie is gained from the comments made by the correspondent for the *Moreton Bay Courier* in April 1848. Glennie had held morning and afternoon services at Ipswich which was depicted as 'this remote village'. The correspondent described the preaching 'as simple in the extreme and admirably adapted for his hearers, being purely scriptural'. Glennie left a substantial legacy still reflected by the churches and schools in the area. In some sources Glennie is referred to as 'the Apostle of the Downs'.

Leslie Mentions Jubbs

In 1847 Patrick Leslie sold Newstead House in Brisbane and his brother, George, negotiated the purchase of the Goomburra Run for Patrick at a price of £1200. In the previous year Jubb applied for a building licence at the Dalrymple crossing.

Patrick Leslie was the best known and for a time the most influential of the early Darling Downs squatters and it would seem that by 1850 he was concerned with both the unrestricted movement of stock across Goomburra and possibly the theft of stock. Leslie expressed his concerns in a *Moreton Bay Courier* notice.

To Persons Travelling Sheep through Darling Downs

NOTICE is hereby given, that any person travelling sheep through the Run of Goomburra by any other Road than the Main Line from Warwick to Drayton, crossing Dalrymple Creek at Jubbs will be prosecuted; as will persons moving Stock from the run without giving notice to the undersigned, or to his Overseer.

Patrick Leslie
Goomburra[9]

It is noted that Leslie refers to the crossing as 'Jubbs' as did Glennie in 1849 and 1852. Jubbs was the most significant and best known building at the crossing. He was still at the crossing during part of 1850 but in that year he obtained the Woolpack Inn. In *Letters to the Colonial Secretary 1848-1850* relating to Moreton Bay there is a return for August 1850 headed Names/Stations/District/etc., and the name William Jubb with the occupation of blacksmith appears but with no link to a station or a location. This information was probably obtained when Jubb was in the process of leaving Dalrymple Creek and setting up at Gap Creek.

Remains of Jubb's Inn

When the surveyor George Pratten completed the survey of Allora in 1859, he identified not just Jubb Street but also a site described as the 'Remains of Jubbs Inn'. This raises the question as to whether Pratten believed that Jubb sold alcohol or was this simply an existing rumour which was perpetuated by using the term 'inn'. William Jubb had a building licence not a liquor licence, but the possibility remains that he periodically sold alcohol. It would be interesting to know what constituted the 'remains' which surveyor Pratten observed and included in his 1859 survey.

Ward-Brown (1988), commenting on information in the Rolleston's record books, notes that the blacksmith's forge at Goomburra was used in subsequent descriptions of the run. She suggests it must have been close to the boundary of Goomburra and the Spicer's Gap road. [10]

At the time of construction, Jubb's building was probably a barn-like structure with vertical split planks and a stringy bark roof. The floor may well have been compounded dirt. An even harder floor could be provided if ant bed material was available in the area.

This was worked into a mortar type mix, spread on the floor and could be up to 6 inches thick.

Buildings such as Jubbs on Dalrymple Creek would be very cold in winter. Various reports appeared in newspapers regarding the size of the fires in early Darling Downs houses and it seemed that these could be up to 8 feet long, 5 feet deep and 6 feet high. (1 foot=30.48cms) With no insulation these fires had to keep the area warm and yet also be suitable for the cooking of meals. A lot of Darling Downs trees disappeared in these fires. In early basic structures such as Jubbs, lighting came from a 'fat light'. This was a tin filled with tallow and a wick for lighting.

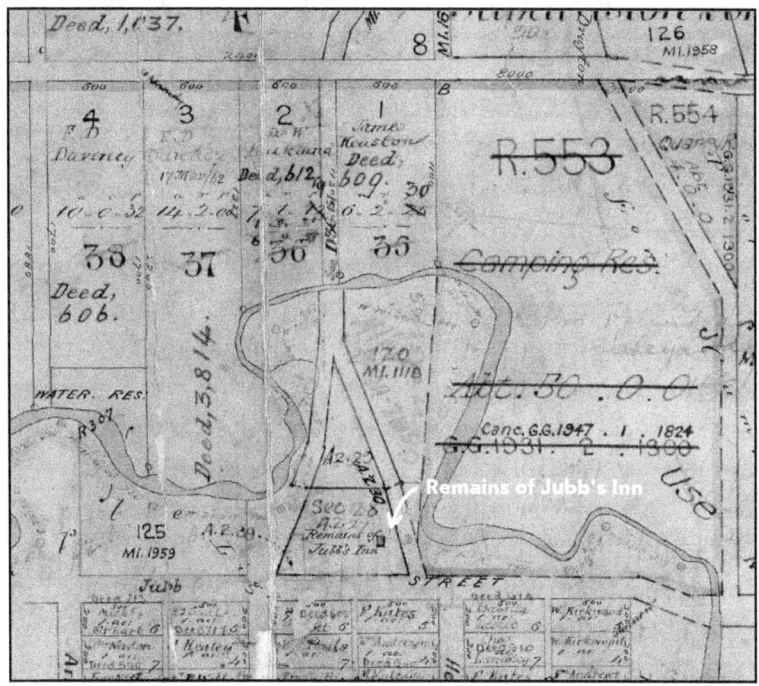

2. Allora Survey by George Pratten, (1859)

Blacksmith's Requirements

Jubb required various materials when he set up as a blacksmith on Dalrymple Creek. The only evidence of where these were obtained was in the cargo list of the steamer *Tamar* which arrived in Brisbane May 1847 and was reported by the *Moreton Bay Courier*.[11]

There was a consignment for Jubb including 77 bars of iron, 6 bundles of iron, 1 parcel of boxes, and one package. Certainly some of this shipment met the needs of a blacksmith. Also included in the Jubb consignment were 3 plough wings. These could be attached to a heavy bar or wooden frame and pulled by a horse or bullock to plough fertile soil near Dalrymple Creek. Later in this text there is mention of Jubb trading agricultural produce with the large Maryland Run, and the question is raised of a possible link between the arrival of the plough wings and the production of agricultural products. Assuming the plough wings were for Jubb's use, two possibilities arise. Jubb either had in mind becoming self-sufficient in an isolated area, or he had an eye on crop production as a means for entering the extensive barter trade that existed in the colony.

On the other hand, the plough wings may have been ordered for another Dalrymple Creek hut owner or for a manager of a nearby run.

There was another item worth noting on the *Tamar* for Jubb. It was '1 hhd' and this translates into 1 hogshead which held 54 gallons (245.5 litres) of alcohol. Both William and George Jubb were known to enjoy an occasional drink. It could be assumed that the hogshead was for the Jubbs and their friends. There remains another possibility. In periods of heavy rain with the creek running a 'banker' the Jubbs may have generously offered bullock drivers, timber-cutters, and shepherds, a 'swig' from the hogshead. Unfortunately this generosity may in reality have been an expensive 'swig'.

Jubb 'A Jack of All Trades'

Little has been written about the life of William Jubb but probably the best known fact about him relates to his time as a publican at Woolpack Inn. The reading of various chapters in *Rosenthal-Historic Shire* does provide a more comprehensive picture of Jubb and surprisingly he is described as a 'jack of all trades'. The indication that Jubb was the only registered builder in the Warwick district until around 1850 and that he may have been involved in the construction of Woolpack Inn for Alphen is tantalising. This question of whether Jubb was a registered builder has already been queried in this text. Perhaps of even greater interest in *Rosenthal* is the data based on access to the records of the large Maryland Run which was initially owned by Matthew Henry Marsh. In 1848 it was estimated that this run was 200,000 acres with a carrying capacity of 25,000 sheep.

Ward-Brown wrote:

> William Jubb received income from Maryland for the sale of 42 bushels of maize at 5/- per bushel £10/10/0d and for the sale of onions for £2/16/8d, and Wm Jubb made part of his payment to John Collins, Publican, Warwick.[12]

Unfortunately the year of the above mentioned Maryland transaction is not recorded in *Rosenthal*.

Jubb's payment from Maryland was not trivial as it represented approximately 30% of what a labourer would receive for a year's work. The 42 bushels of maize translates into just over 2,000 generic sized maize cobs (ears) and it is assumed that £2/16/8d translates into a lot of onions. It would seem that Jubb owed some money to the publican at Warwick. Could it be possible that Jubb occasionally purchased a few dozen bottles or even a hogshead from Collins? This may have been used by the Dalrymple Creek blacksmith to keep the weary travellers happy as they went on their journeys.

It is speculation as to where these agricultural products originated from. Jubb was a blacksmith and he was involved in building. He may not have grown the maize and onions but could have been involved in some barter arrangement for work completed.

The records held in the *NSW Archives* indicate that John Collins held the first licence for the Horse and Jockey Hotel at Warwick in 1849 and that Catherine Collins held the licence in 1853 and 1854. John Collins was again the licensee in 1856 and 1857. It seems highly likely that a member of the Collins family held the licence of this hotel from 1849 to 1857. In 1849 Jubb was at the Dalrymple Creek crossing (Allora) and for the other years at the Woolpack Inn. The Jubb trade with Maryland would have occurred when Jubb was at the Dalrymple crossing rather than when he had moved further away to Gap Creek.

The State Library of Queensland holds in their heritage collection records of Maryland Run. A search of these records was conducted and even with the help of volunteer research assistance the names of Jubb and Collins could not be located. The task is cognitively demanding as there are hundreds of pages of financial records.

The colony of NSW was a convenient dumping ground for convicts but virtually no attention was paid to the establishment of an appropriate currency system. The immense shortage of cash and notes ensured the introduction of a barter and promissory note economy in the colony. Jubb's involvement in possible barter at Maryland Run was just an example of what was taking place. The other possibility is that Jubb received payment in maize and vegetables for work completed as a blacksmith. He then 'cashed' these in at Maryland Run.

(Note: See clarification regarding the source of produce sold to Maryland Run in the Postscript, page 116.)

Alphen at Woolpack Inn

It is known that Jubb left Dalrymple Creek and moved to Woolpack Inn at Gap Creek where Henry Alphen had initially established the inn. The precise details of this move are somewhat cloudy and may be more comprehensible with a brief consideration of Alphen's association with the inn.

Alphen arrived in New South Wales as a convict. By 1847 he was a stockman for Patrick Leslie and reported that he had found a better route from the Darling Downs to Ipswich than either the Cunningham or Gorman gaps. He received reward money from the government and the simple story was that he used this money to build the Woolpack Inn at Gap Creek. How much he received as a reward is not known. There is another view that the reward money was used by Alphen to establish a boiling down works on the Condamine, a project that failed.

Alphen did not hold the first liquor licence for Woolpack Inn. Data from the *New South Wales Archives* indicate that on 5 January 1848 a licence was granted for the Woolpack Inn in the name of James Fortune and was renewed on 21 June, 1848. Who was James Fortune?

He certainly spent part of his time as an innkeeper in Sydney. In 1856 he held the liquor licence for John Bull Inn in King's Street Sydney and in 1858 the licence for The Dock Inn, Balmain. Fortune continued an involvement in Sydney hotels, building the Star Hotel and prior to this held the licence for the Forth and Clyde Hotel in Balmain.

There was concern about James Fortune's application for the John Bull Inn in 1854 as the *Illustrated Sydney News* indicated his application for the inn was refused. Other sources claim he gained the licence in 1854 but had paid £1000 for the licence during the year and this was illegal. If this is true, Fortune was not short of money. It is likely that in 1848 Fortune was the nominee for the Woolpack Inn while the hands-on work was being carried out by Alphen.

Sociocultural Considerations

Jubb and his wife were living at the Woolpack Inn during the 1850s in what could only be described as a rudimentary society. There were sharp divisions between the new arrivals and the indigenous people. Books by Connors (2015) *Warrior* and Hansford (2016) *The Elusive Archibald Young* indicate how frequent and serious the 'divisions' were between the Aboriginal population and the new settlers in parts of the Moreton Bay and Darling Downs districts. These divisions also existed between the 'haves' and the 'have nots'. The 'haves' were the government officials and landowners such as the squatters. The 'have nots' were labourers, many with convict backgrounds, and seemingly free-settlers arriving to fill labour gaps created by the end of transportation. In rural areas such as Moreton Bay and Darling Downs a number of these new arrivals were contracted or indentured labourers.

Legal, medical, educational and communication facilities were at best spartan in the rural areas of the colony. Administrators may have held generalised, but poorly developed objectives relating to equality and justice in the 1850s. On a number of occasions the administrators were far removed from, or completly missed the targets of equality and justice.

There are always some legal actions that sound quite peculiar, even bizarre, and this was evident in an 1854 case. In May 1854 the Jubbs had been at the Woolpack Inn for nearly four years when the *Moreton Bay Courier* reported the Liqua case which was heard at the Brisbane Circuit Court. The Jubbs were not involved in the case but the accused, an indentured Chinese shepherd named Liqua, mentioned their names. The charge of assault was brought forward by Edward Wienholt. He argued that Liqua had struck him in the face with a bolt after being told that he had brought his stock in too early. Liqua's evidence, given with the assistance of an interpreter, was rambling, disjointed and often unrelated to the assault charge. He claimed that he had not been paid recently by Wienholt's brother and that this person had tied him up and flogged him. He had also chased him while on horseback and cut Liqua's shoulder with a sword. Liqua reported that his master had forced him to pay £2/10/- to get the wound attended to by a surgeon. He had shown this wound to the Jubbs at the Woolpack Inn and they said it was 'no good'. The charge was dismissed.

Slocomb, in her book *Among Australian Pioneers*, interprets the case of Liqua as the court being so shocked by the demonstrably true accusations by Liqua that a verdict of not guilty was immediately returned. She continued that there is no record of redress regarding wages, let alone punishment of the powerful squatter for his torture of Liqua. Whether the interpretation of Liqua's case by Slocomb is correct or not may be debatable. The reality is that colonial Australia was based on an authoritarian model which had as one of its foundation principles a master-servant association modelled on that operating in the United Kingdom and Europe. The Jubbs and many like them lived in a harsh and at times violent environment.

Jubb Acquires the Woolpack Inn

There are variations in the story as to how Jubb obtained the Woolpack Inn. Lands Commissioner Rolleston granted Alphen a building licence and this was for construction purposes on land apparently obtained from the Leslie brothers. Some say the money Alphen used to build the inn came from the reward he obtained as a consequence of locating the new route. At a later date Jubb said he purchased the inn directly from Alphen in 1850. The Warwick magistrates had granted a general liquor licence for the inn, and Jubb reported he spent £500 getting the premises in order. Some reports identify the Leslie brothers as performing significant roles in relation to virtually all business dealings relating to the Woolpack Inn up till the commencement of the Jubb era. It is difficult to be precise regarding the roles performed by the Leslies at the Woolpack Inn. They did, however, push for the development of a village in the area where the inn was located. There was a lack of continuing support for this proposal at the official decision making levels. In simple terms there were other locations, more in need, and better suited for the development of a village in the surrounding districts.

The fact that the Cunninghams Gap inn was called the Woolpack Inn by Alphen, or perhaps the Leslies, indicates that an embryonic development associated with wool was under way in the mid to late 1840s. This projected development was evidenced in various other locations in the colony of NSW as quite a number of inns named the Woolpack sprung up.

It was a fortuitous decision by Jubb to move from Dalrymple Creek to Gap Creek. In October 1851 the *Moreton Bay Courier* reported that the value of tallow exported from Brisbane was approximately double the value of exported wool. By July 1859 the *Moreton Bay Courier* indicated the value of wool exported was around six times the value of exported tallow. The 'wool money' attracted all types of businesses. Tradesmen were required, roads required improvement, and timber was needed for the new developments. As the saying goes Jubb certainly had the opportunity 'to ride on the sheep's back'.

Jubb was at Woolpack Inn until mid-1859 and for part of this period his brother George was a blacksmith and wheelwright at the inn. Newspaper reports were such that at times George may not have been of great assistance to his brother. There are questions as to where the Jubb brothers acquired their knowledge of the skills required to become blacksmiths and wheelwrights. They may have had formal training but in the then isolated areas such as Goomburra and Gap Creek it would be no surprise if these enterprising brothers made the most of on the job training.

The first Mrs Jubb (Margaret) had a major involvement in the operation of the inn, but in 1855 she was killed in an accident while seeking medical assistance. Jubb remarried a woman named Eleanor Sherriff in 1857 and they had a son, Cephas William Jubb in 1858. The Christian names of this son were sometimes presented as William Cephas. There is lack of precise knowledge about Jubb's second wife except that by 1861 the gloss of the marriage had totally faded.

Jubb's Religious Affiliations

The Woolpack innkeeper's full name was William Cephas Jubb. The name Cephas is used in the Aramaic language and translated means rock or stone. Jesus called the apostle Simon Peter, Cephas, because he was the rock upon which the Christian church was to be built. When Cephas is translated into Greek it becomes Petros and in English it becomes Peter. Several sources have suggested that the name Cephas was more common among Roman Catholics than those from any other Church. The use of Cephas could suggest Jubb's parents, or at least one of them, adhered to Catholic teachings.

Following the burial of Margaret Jubb in a non-Catholic section, Jubb had her body exhumed and reburied in a correctly consecrated Catholic burial area. In following years Jubb made donations to the Catholic Church at Ipswich, perhaps for the assistance associated with exhuming Margaret's body.

No evidence was located of Jubb being a 'church-goer' but I am sure he would not have been impressed by the relative who arranged for a Church of England minister to speak at his graveside.

Perceptions of the Jubbs

Two visitors to the Woolpack Inn commented on Jubb and his first wife Margaret. These were Reverend Henry Stobart and businessman Nehemiah Bartley. Stobart was the tutor of two young English Lords touring the area in 1852. He described Margaret as a 'little, diminutive and ugly woman'. Stobart also considered her 'unduly polite and loquacious'. She became aggressive with Lord Schomberg-Kerr for curing a bandicoot skin in the hand basin at Woolpack Inn. Schomberg apparently then showed great dislike for 'the old lady'. 'Old' hardly seemed the correct term to describe Margaret Jubb as in 1852 she was only 32 years old. Differences of opinion occurred and the Darling Downs historian Hall, writing in 1925 contended that pioneer women passing over the range found Jubb's Inn a 'worldly heaven' and Margaret as a 'sympathetic' and 'kindly woman'. As we know, perception is in the eye of the beholder.

It was during the visit by Stobart and the two English Lords, Henry Scott Montagu and Schomberg-Kerr, that Montagu commenced a watercolour entitled Mrs Jubb's public house, 1853. No doubt Jubb was delighted that a painting of the Woolpack Inn was undertaken. He may have been less impressed with the title which described the inn as being the property of Mrs Jubb.

3. Painting of Mrs Jubb's Public House, (Montagu 1853)

The much travelled businessman and story teller, Nehemiah Bartley, had two books published *Opals and Agates* (1892) and *Australian Pioneers and Reminiscences* (1896). These books contained stories about many of the early settlers on the Darling Downs including Jubb. Bartley met Jubb on a few occasions and described him as 'a brawny bit of stuff'. He further suggested that Jubb was a 'character' who was 'illiterate', 'rough and aggressive in appearance' and had, 'an oily emollient voice'. Jubb apparently endeavoured to use complex words, but not always successfully. One story was about Jubb walking back to the inn on a very hot day. He encountered a hostile group of Aborigines and used sign language to explain that his men were following with wheel barrows full of supplies. The hostile group rushed off to intercept the supplies. Jubb apparently told Bartley that he did not tell them the supply party was well armed. This story was improved when Bartley suggested that not only was it extremely hot and the slope severe, but that Jubb was walking uphill with his pants over his shoulder. Given the considerable conflict between the original land owners and the European seekers of land it is surprising that the above account is the only 'aboriginal story' linked to Jubb located during the search for information. Unfortunately the intention of the story was to provide humour while ignoring a potential outcome of death or injury to some indigenous dwellers.

Harry Bracker was the son of Fred Bracker, an early settler and authority regarding sheep. Harry wrote a number of reminiscences regarding the Darling Downs and these appeared in various newspapers. One appeared in the *Warwick Daily News* in 1922 depicting Jubb as a typical

John Bull, portly and partial to a glass of beer. By way of contrast, Bracker described Mrs Jubb as an energetic Irish woman always on the go. She criticised Jubb for time wasting and on one occasion Jubb was reported as saying 'my wife is of a hostile temperament'.[13]

When the Reverend William Ridley recounted that he called at the Woolpack in 1855 he did not mention the Jubbs. However, like many other early visitors, he did comment on the almost impenetrable scrub along 'the road' to the inn.

The Woolpack was in an isolated area. If riding toward Ipswich the next accommodation was the Bush Inn on Warrill Creek in the Fassifern. This inn was approximately a 25 mile horse ride away and a similar riding distance when moving on to Warwick. Distances then recorded are now difficult to estimate as the old tracks sought out good creek crossings, avoided thick scrub patches, sharp inclines, known swampy areas and even locations where Aboriginal attacks had occurred.

Arnold Wienholt

In 1848 Arnold Wienholt arrived in Sydney and took over the Strathmillar (Maryvale) Run in 1849. The portion of land where the Woolpack Inn stood was on this run and in a very short period of time Jubb was in conflict with Wienholt. By December 1851 the *Sydney Morning Herald* reported that there had been a hearing by the Warwick magistrates ordering Wienholt to pay Jubb £9/19/-for a specified debt.[14]

The reason for this debt is not known. Wienholt paid the amount under protest and then sued Jubb for the same amount. At the hearing by the magistrates, Wienholt wanted to provide his own defence for the claimed debt but this was rejected. It was ruled that this second case could not be heard as it constituted a second hearing for the same debt. Despite an appeal to the Supreme Court this seemingly strange legal decision was not changed. Justices Roger Therry and John Dickinson considered the refusal by the magistrates to allow Wienholt to provide a defence somewhat unusual but it seems that this was where the case was concluded.

The 1851 case regarding the debt was the first noted incident of the major disagreement between Jubb and Wienholt. For several years there was a festering dispute over ownership of the block of land and the structures built on that land known as Woolpack Inn. It was not until mid-1859 that this dispute reached a legal conclusion.

Margaret Jubb

In April of 1855 the *Moreton Bay Courier* reported that Mrs Jubb had been very ill and Jubb decided to take her down to Ipswich and then on to Brisbane for medical treatment. She was placed in a horse-drawn dray but during the trip the wheel hit a stump and overturned. Although Mrs Jubb was killed in the accident, it was decided to report the accident to the correct authorities. William Jubb's brother George was sent on to Ipswich while William sat in the pouring rain with his deceased wife. When the total party eventually arrived at Ipswich a decision was made to hold a funeral in an Episcopalian section of a cemetery. This was when things really started to go wrong. The first grave was too shallow, too short and too narrow. Adjustments were made. A priest who was in attendance refused to conduct the service in a Protestant grave area. Mrs Jubb was later exhumed and laid to rest with the appropriate rituals of her church. However, this was not the end of the saga surrounding Margaret Jubb. When George Jubb went for assistance, contact was made with two doctors, Frederick Cumming and Henry Challinor. Dr Cumming actually went to the site of the accident with Constable

John Laidler, but both doctors sent letters to the *Moreton Bay Courier* explaining their actions on that wet night. Dr Challinor thought his 'want of humanity' was being questioned.[15]

Following his wife's death, Jubb placed a letter in the newspaper to 'the inhabitants of Ipswich'. This thank you letter to all living in the Ipswich area commences and concludes with the word 'Gentlemen'. This form of address was an indication of where the world was regarding issues of equality rather than an indictment of Jubb. He first thanked those who attended the grave site. In particular, Jubb thanked Mrs Mercer of the Bush Inn who attended his wife the day before the accident. He also noted the 'humane and considerate attention' of Patrick O'Sullivan and John Clune.[16]

It is probable that those specifically mentioned by Jubb in his letter were friends or associates. The Mercers and John Clune were like Jubb, in that they were lessees of inns. Mercers experienced financial difficulties at the Bush Inn (Fassifern) and tragically lost their daughter during a flood in 1855. John Clune was lessee of the Shearers Arms and then the Claire Castle Hotel in Ipswich during the 1850s. He later became a councillor in Ipswich. Patrick O'Sullivan, an Irish convict, was a successful land owner and business man in Ipswich who became a member of the Queensland Legislative Assembly.

There was one other rather pointed comment in Jubb's letter to the people of Ipswich. He wrote about how difficult it was regarding

... incidences of sympathy. On all hands, but with one exception, in your township I have met with it in such measure that it must ever remain in my grateful remembrances.[17]

The above extract appears to imply that of all the people Jubb met, only one in the Ipswich township, did not express sympathy regarding the death of Margaret Jubb.

Two years after the exhuming of Margaret Jubb, Father William McGinty, a Catholic priest at Ipswich, thanked Jubb for his donation of £1 to the Ipswich Church. He further pointed out that Jubb had made several such donations and it is possible that this generosity may have been related to the earlier exhuming and reburial of Margaret Jubb. The *Freeman's Journal* reported in July 1858 that Jubb donated £5 to an appeal organised by Father McGinty to erect a church in Warwick.

Horses Stolen and Wallet Lost

Horse theft was a common occurrence in the early days of colonial Australia. In regions where distances travelled were often great, horses were the major means of moving around. In the Cunninghams Gap area not all properties were completely fenced. The terrain was rugged, large patches of dense scrub existed and there was a shortage of police officers. These factors enhanced the prospects of people intent on stealing horses. Newspapers contained a number of reward notices concerning horses that either disappeared or were stolen. Jubb, at his isolated inn, offered rewards for horses apparently stolen in 1854 and 1855. A £5 reward was offered for one horse stolen 'from Jubb's door'. The other horse was distinctively marked and had a branding of JW. This horse was reportedly stolen or strayed and £10 was offered for its return.

It is doubtful if 1855 was a good year for Jubb. His wife had been killed in a dray accident and his horse had disappeared. In September of 1855 the *Moreton Bay Courier* reported that Jubb visited Ipswich and called in at the Queens Arms Hotel, probably for a meal and possibly for a drink or two. George Thorn was listed as gaining a licence for the historic Queens Arms Hotel in 1844 but by 1855 the licensee was James McDonald. Following this visit to the Queens Arms, Jubb again inserted a £10 reward notice in the newspaper. It seems he may have lost his wallet in the bar but he really believed it had been stolen. The wallet contained notes, cheques and orders to the value of £109. Payment was stopped on the cheques and orders but the notes were unsecured. There is no mention in following newspapers of a claimant for the reward.[18]

Trips to Sydney

Jubb did make a number of trips to Sydney during his time as the licensee of the Woolpack Inn. Those with the financial resources travelled on the steamers to Sydney in personal cabins. The others were treated like sardines and 'housed' downstairs somewhere in what was referred to as steerage. On such Sydney trips the Irish blacksmith and innkeeper moved among the 'more significant' people of the colony. Certainly some of these trips were to do with legal issues. For example, in 1857 Jubb sent a petition to Colonel George Barney, the then Commissioner of Crown Lands, regarding his dispute with Wienholt over ownership of the Woolpack Inn. It is highly likely Jubb required not only legal advice for this petition but also substantial support in writing up the document. This petition was sent from Garrick's Head Inn, York Street, Sydney where Alphen held liquor licences.

Trips to Sydney were made by Jubb in 1851, 1853, 1856, 1857 and 1860. There were probably other years when Jubb visited Sydney and not all appeared to have a strictly business focus. In some years Jubb made two trips to Sydney and this certainly occurred in 1857. During 1857

Jubb's first trip to Sydney departed Moreton Bay 10 February arriving in Sydney on the 12 February and the second trip occurring in May. The February 1857 trip to Sydney and then on to Parramatta could best be described as a comprehensive shambles. The details of this first trip to Sydney in 1857, including Jubb's evidence, made more than interesting reading in the *Sydney Morning Herald* on Saturday 23 May 1857. This article presented a picture of bad women, alcohol, robbery, violence, drugs, illness and severe prison sentences. In summary the Irish innkeeper had a very rough time and may have left Sydney for Moreton Bay on the first available steamer.[19]

Shambles at Parramatta

At the Court of Quarter Sessions in Parramatta Jubb explained he had reason to go to Sydney in February carrying a great deal of money in £5 notes. He took up lodgings at Hack's Rose and Crown public house in Parramatta. This is now a historic public house that commenced around 1823 and is still operating in 2018. The text contains a photograph of the Rose and Crown as it was somewhere between 1870 and 1890.[20]

In court that day were Joseph Reynolds, Margaret Reynolds, John Haigh, Ellen Haigh and James Goody. These good citizens of Parramatta were jointly and severally indicted for stealing from Jubb. On his first night at the Rose and Crown, Jubb, being a generous man, shouted Margaret Reynolds and Ellen Haigh a few glasses of spirits. Mrs Hack, knowing the character of the two women, asked Jubb not to bring them into her public house. Jubb decided to buy a bottle of gin and went outside with the women. He also informed the court that he was feeling rather poorly. Did this mean he was already drunk? Jubb decided to sit down on the road with the women. Margaret Reynolds put her hand in Jubb's pocket and took his wallet containing £45. Jubb explained that the women then decoyed him to a house where there were three males who 'hocussed' him with a drink. [Hocussed= to deceive and stupefy with a drug.] Assuming the accuracy of Jubb's evidence he was in very poor shape. He stated that he 'almost immediately fell senseless', was 'ill all the next day', had a 'swollen tongue' almost 'preventing his power of speech', 'the crown of his head was rising and falling', he experienced 'violent agony' and was 'refused water'.

When Jubb began to recover, he found his gold watch hidden under a cup and was also relieved that the attackers had not found the thirteen £5 notes he had hidden in a silk handkerchief tied around his leg. The silk handkerchief trick may have been a Jubb special or perhaps it was a proven way to hide money when travelling in the 1850s. As a Chief Constable caught three of the accused spending £5 notes, it was relatively easy for the jury to reach a guilty verdict. The two females were sentenced to two years hard labour in Parramatta goal and the Chief Constable reported that these women were as bad as they could possibly be. Joseph Reynolds received a similar two year sentence in Parramatta goal and James Goody an eighteen month sentence. John Haigh had a reduced sentence of six months as he was able to produce a letter of previous good character.

It is difficult to explain why Jubb carried a considerable sum of money on his trip to Sydney and then out to Parramatta where he became involved in a messy incident. One of the possibilities was that the trip was undertaken with alcohol and women in mind. The current world with objectives such as equality and

4. Rose and Crown Hotel Parramatta. (1870-1890).

Weekend NOTES, 28 September 2015, reported this hotel was built by Robert 'One-Armed' Green who lost his limb in 1815 at the Battle of Waterloo. He is buried next door at the All Saints Church.

respect for women was not the world Jubb existed in during the 1840s to 1860s. It is possible that Jubb held quite pragmatic reasons why a wife could be useful at the inn. His first wife, Margaret, was a hard worker in both the kitchen and bar and it is highly likely he hoped that a replacement could cope with such work. If she could cut wood for the inn that would also help. The possibility could well have crossed his mind that on cold and misty nights near the crest of Cunninghams Gap a wife would help keep his bed warm.

The 1850s in the colony of NSW was a time when it was rather unsafe to carry large sums of money with you. A large proportion of the population were ex-convicts and there were insufficient number of constables to enforce the law. Despite this, Jubb, in 1855 at the Queens Arms, Ipswich, and 1857 at the Rose and Crown, Parramatta, was involved in incidents when he was carrying in excess of £100. This did demonstrate that he had the capacity to earn considerable amounts of money and not everyone was convinced about the safety of banks. Townships like Ipswich and Warwick had banks but there was a suspicion about 'your' money being held and looked after, by 'others'.

Other Business

In 1857 Jubb made his second trip to Sydney by steamer and arrived on 12 May. On 21 May he was involved in the trial at Parramatta. By 4 June he had made his way out to Windsor where he married a widow, Eleanor Sherriff (nee Eleanor Robinson) who was 37 years old. Her first husband Richard Sherriff died in 1853 and they had an 8 year old daughter named Elizabeth Jane. Jubb and the new wife and daughter returned to Brisbane on 22 June. It is noted that the daughter was referred to as Miss Jubb by the *Moreton Bay Courier*. The Jubbs probably made bookings for themselves and their daughter. It may have been assumed by those accepting the booking that she was a Jubb when in reality she was Miss Sherriff.

We can only speculate about when Jubb actually met Eleanor Sherriff. Their courtship may have developed over a considerable period of time. Alternatively it may have been love at first sight during the May to June trip of 1857. It would indeed have been fascinating to know how Jubb rationally explained the events which occurred in the March 'shambles at Parramatta' to his new wife Eleanor.

Jubb was away from the Woolpack for a number of weeks in 1857 and it is assumed that his brother George took over the running of the inn. Such a decision may have created some anxiety as George, like his brother, had a fondness for alcohol. It is possible that Jubb's servant, James Kelly, was in charge. Given that 12 months later Kelly claimed Jubb threatened to kill him such a decision may be questioned.

Servants at the Woolpack

It was probably always difficult to get first class servants in the 1840s and 1850s. However, living at the Woolpack Inn, a remote location near the Cunninghams Gap, both Alphen and Jubb experienced unusual problems with servants.

Before Jubb took over the Woolpack Inn the first incident of potential violence occurred there in 1848. Alphen had employed William Meara, an Irish born convict, as a servant. Apparently Meara got very drunk one night. He threatened those at the inn with a knife and demanded they give him powder and shot. He was charged with an act of violence and the case against him was heard at Warwick. The case was dismissed as it was decided that the incident was not in keeping with Meara's previous behaviour and character. However, when the Bench examined Meara's documents it was discovered that he had been employed by Alphen under the Masters and Servants Act and his application included a forged record of his discharge as a convict. Meara received a sentence of three months hard labour in a Sydney goal.

James Kelly was employed as a servant by Jubb around 1855. During that time Kelly gave evidence against John Flood, alias Jefferies, who was involved in a case concerning a stolen bridle, saddle and horse. Nothing more was heard about Kelly until he charged Jubb with attempting to shoot him. This case was heard by John Douglas at the Warwick Magistrate's court and reported in the *Moreton Bay Courier* 30 October 1858. Kelly had words with Jubb's brother, George, the morning of the alleged assault. On that same morning Kelly assaulted a man called McAuley. Kelly said he told William Jubb he was leaving in a week and a scuffle followed. Jubb collected his 'stick gun' and during the scuffle the gun was knocked from Jubb's hands and Kelly took it to Chief Constable Thomas McEvoy's house. John Douglas, a squatter and magistrate, heard the case at Warwick and said it had been made out to his satisfaction and he sentenced Jubb to six months in a Brisbane goal and his stick gun was forfeited.[21]

The decision of the Warwick Magistrates Court was challenged less than a month later. Jubb's legal representative in Brisbane, Daniel Foley Roberts, made an application for a writ of *habeas corpus* in the Supreme Court at Brisbane and this was granted. The *Moreton Bay Courier* 24 November 1858 reported that Judge Samuel Milford then had Jubb attend the court and following an address by Roberts and an examination of various papers Milford ruled that Jubb had been illegally confined.[22]

French in his book *Pubs, Ploughs & Peculiar People* (1982) suggested that 'Jubb was given to impetuous violence'. This was probably correct and Jubb had certainly experienced the highs and lows of the then legal system. Following the Supreme Court decision Jubb is likely to have made a hasty return to the Woolpack Inn; even desisting on this occasion from making a quick call to the Queens Arms in Ipswich.

There was jealousy between the emerging towns of Drayton and Warwick and the *Moreton Bay Courier* in 1859 reported that Warwick was organising John Douglas, a squatter from Talgai, to stand in the general election. This did not impress all and the following paragraph appeared in the newspaper:

> Mr Douglas is anything but liked. His haughty imperious manner and aristocratic notions, his disbelief in the powers of the people, his extreme squattocratic opinions and his recent judgement upon the man Jubb, have tended to produce this antagonistic feeling.[23]

Actually Douglas seems to have had a complex political career and was more liberal and amenable in many of his beliefs than a number of his squatter associates. In 1877 he became Premier of Queensland for nearly two years.

Jubb Brothers and Alcohol

George Jubb, a blacksmith, was at Allora and also at Woolpack Inn. Well this is what is written in a couple of publications but it is difficult to precisely locate a primary source indicating George's arrival and departure from Allora. As mentioned previously George was cited in the *Moreton Bay Courier* several times for his unsatisfactory behaviour. There is little doubt that William Jubb enjoyed a drink or two but his brother George's drinking was such that he made various appearances before the court. These appearances were first mentioned in the 1850s. One charge was at Ipswich where he was he fined 5/- or 24 hours in goal for being drunk and disorderly in the streets. Another occurred at Brisbane where the 20/- fine was for being drunk and disorderly in the streets and for using obscene language. The third fine was £2 or seven days in prison at Dalby. In this case the fine was for obscene language.

William Jubb certainly drank in the bar of the Woolpack Inn and he had rather unusual incidents at the Queens Arms, Ipswich and the Rose and Crown, Parramatta. Another case relating to inns and publicans provided an even clearer picture of William Jubb. The *Moreton Bay*

Courier reported on a Supreme Court hearing before Judge Alfred Lutwyche in August 1859 involving two publicans. The publicans were Jubb from the Woolpack Inn and Patrick Fleming the licensee of the Downs Hotel in Warwick. Other than being a publican, Fleming was active in the purchase and sale of land in the Warwick district.[24] He had an interesting background as in 1849 the Court of Petty Sessions at Warwick described him as a cabinet maker and granted him a licence as a hawker and peddler.

The court case was reported in the newspapers as an action to recover two cheques. These cheques totalled £18/13/2 and it became apparent that Jubb had been drinking at the time the cheques were signed. One witness, Godfrey O'Rourke, said that he could not swear that the cheques had been drawn by Jubb but they looked like the way he wrote when he was drunk. O'Rourke was a successful businessman who at various times owned a carrier business and a building where auctions could be held. It is noted that from 1855 to 1859 he held the licence for an Ipswich inn with the delightful name of the Cottage of Content. It is highly likely that Jubb was known at this particular inn. Mr Edward Stanley Ebsworth, the manager of the Joint Stock Bank, stated that he did not think the signatures were those of Jubb and that they should not be accepted. Neither Jubb nor Fleming banked at the Joint Stock Bank and it is assumed Ebsworth was called as an independent witness.

Many of the early writs held by the Queensland State Archives are a few pages in length. The Fleming v Jubb document contains 23 pages of what in layman terms

5. Signatures Extracted from Cheques and Supreme Court Writ. (Cheques June 1858 and Affidavit March 1859).

would represent claim and counter claims. Lutwyche felt that the cause of the case 'was not of sufficient value to justify the action of the Supreme Court'. This did not stop the case going ahead and the jury found for the plaintiff an amount of £18/13/2 believing that the defendant Jubb wrote the cheques and knew what he was doing. Jubb had submitted a sworn affidavit on 13 March 1859 before the Commissioner for Affidavits, Warwick claiming the exact opposite. A part of the submitted affidavit is reproduced below:

> If the said cheques or either of them be in my hand writing the same were signed at a time when I was so drunken, intoxicated and under the influence of liquor and thereby deprived of some understanding and the use of my reason, as to be unable to understand or comprehend the meaning, object, nature or effect thereof.
>
> William Jubb

It should be noted that the two cheques used to pay Fleming at his Warwick inn were signed with a scrawly Jubb signature. However Fleming's name was printed on the cheque. This appeared to be an interesting business practice of allowing the clients to drink and then requiring payment with pre-prepared cheques. This minimised what those lacking in writing skills had to do. It is highly likely that this incident involving signatures created considerable animosity between the two publicans.

In the above-mentioned case, the witness O'Rourke suggested that the signatures on the cheques were just the way Jubb wrote when he was drunk. The year after the case with Fleming, the editor of the *Moreton Bay Courier*, who had the excellent name of Theophilus Parsons Pugh, communicated with Jubb complaining about his writing. Pugh's short and to the point letter appeared in the newspaper and read as follows:

> **William Jubb** – If you would be kind enough to forward your advertisement in more decipherable hieroglyphics, we shall feel obliged.

Earlier in this text it was reported that Nehemiah Bartley thought Jubb was illiterate but perhaps the expression semi-literate was a more accurate description of his capacities. His writing was at best very rough around the edges and Pugh, an experienced reader of handwriting, could not make sense of an advertisement submitted by Jubb.

Jubb's Bank Account

The two cheques drawn by Jubb to pay Fleming were made out to the Bank of Australasia, Ipswich and a search was conducted to establish whether any bank records remained relating to these two inn keepers. The answer was yes, in the ANZ Bank's archive in Victoria. Jubb's account contained 45 entries between 1856 and 1858 and Fleming's account 14 entries between 1857 and 1858. Unfortunately both records cease before the date of the disputed cheques. The following is a summary of Jubb's account. An amount of detail has been deleted, such as daily balances. However, the highest balance evidenced in the remaining entries of Jubb's account was £219/3/11 on 17 December 1857. The comparable balance for Fleming was £488/10/- on 19 January 1858.

It is highly unlikely that the remaining bank records reflect the total reality of Jubb's largely cash business. The bank records of Jubb cover a period of 19 months yet only ten cash deposits occurred during this period. Five of these deposits are described as 'cash' and these reflect Jubb or another authorised person depositing cash at Ipswich. It was a long hard ride for Jubb at Woolpack Inn to reach the Ipswich bank and then return. It would

Date		Particulars	Dr			Cr		
			£	s	d	£	s	d
1856								
Aug	12	Hunter & Co	22					
Aug	14	Platt & Co	3					
Aug	14	Vowels	15					
Aug	15	Gorry	2					
Aug	18	Vowels	1					
Aug	18	Vowels	2					
Aug	18	Vowels	3					
Aug	19	Gill	16					
Sept	1	Cribb	1					
Sept	6	Cash				91	18	4
Oct	30	Cash				42	15	0
Nov	1	Hudson	5					
Nov	19	Yates Chq Dishonour	9	16	6			
Dec	13	Cash				85	11	4
Dec	17	Cash				13	6	10
1857								
Jan	16	Self	150					
Jan	24	Yates Cheque				9	16	6
April	15	Self	10					
April	29	Cash				44	7	3
June	29	Self	70					
July	13	Passbook		1	6			
July	29	Berkmann *	3					
Sept	5	Cash / Post				33	8	5
Oct	26	Self	10					
Oct	29	Wilson & Co	1					
Nov	12	Balbi	3					
Nov	19	Cash / Post				30	11	8
Dec	9	Cash / Letter				38	10	1
1858								
Jan	22	Cash / Letter				36	1	7
Jan	29	Cash / Letter				21	15	3
Mar	1	Cribb & F	4					
Mar	2	Bearer	3					
Mar	3	Wilson & Co	10					
Mar	8	Macalister	2	2				
Mar	9	Gray & Co	4					
Mar	9	Jones & Co	1					
Mar	12	Wilson & Co	22					
Mar	13	Bailie	38	10				
Mar	13	Self	5					
Mar	15	No 29	5					
Mar	19	..aley	2					

6. Transactions in Jubb's bank account (Aug 1856 - Mar 1858).
* Note: Berkman is the correct spelling but other sources use Berkmann or Birkman.

not be unusual for such a ride to be broken by overnight stays at the Bush Inn, Fassifern.

There are five deposits described as 'cash per post' or 'cash per letter'. Despite these deposits being entered as 'cash' they are most likely cheques made out by people who owed Jubb money.

Jubb's bank entries provide an historic snapshot of business transactions evidenced in Ipswich and part of the Southern Downs during the period 1856 to 1858. The names involved were Hunter & Co, Platt & Co, Vowles, Gorry, Gill, Cribb & Co, Cribb & F, Hudson, Berkmann (Berkman), Yates, Gray & Co, Wilson & Co, Balbi, Bailie, Macalister, Gray & Co and Jones & Co. One six letter name lacked clarity but the last four letters are '...aley'. Some of these names reflect substantial links with the history of Ipswich and Warwick and each will be commented on briefly. An exception to these brief comments relates to the consideration of the transactions involving Fleming, Gorry and Berkman. These transactions throw some light on the manner in which specific early Warwick businessmen engaged in financial deals. This consideration seemed relevant to Jubb as in 1862 Fleming engages in another surprising business deal involving Jubb's property.

1856

August 12 (Hunter & Co) Hunter & Co were builders in Ipswich and were paid £22 by Jubb.

August 14 (Platt & Co) Platt & Co ran a drapery store and received £3 from Jubb. In 1854 this firm was named Reeve, Platt & Co and in 1856 it became Crosland & Platt.

August 14 (Vowles) William Vowles, an ex-convict, is usually described as an Ipswich builder and pit-sawyer at Pine Mountain. He certainly was involved in the construction of a number of early Ipswich buildings, but in an 1851 court case (R v Scully [1851] NSWSupCMB45) his occupation was given as a cooper. Jubb made four payments to Vowles totalling £21 in August. As Jubb was also involved in building he may have employed Hunter and Vowles to work on one of his projects. Alternatively he may have employed these builders to do repairs or extensions at the Woolpack Inn.

August 15 (Gorry) Christopher Gorry, an Ipswich saddler, was paid £2 in 1856.

August 19 (Gill) Richard Gill was the post master at Ipswich but combined this with the keeping of a general store. Gill apparently 'sold everything from sugar to flour to a bullock bell'. He was paid £16 by Jubb in 1856.

September 1 (Cribb and Cribb & F) Benjamin Cribb and John Clarke Foote commenced a business known as Cribb & Foote. This was a leading department store in Ipswich that lasted 125 years until the premises was destroyed by fire in 1985. The history of Ipswich is deeply interwoven with this business and these two men. Jubb paid £5 to this business between 1856 and 1857.

November 1 (Hudson) Frederick Hudson moved from Sydney to Ipswich and established himself as a tailor. In 1856 Jubb paid him £5. He was distracted by the gold rush near Mudgee but returned to Ipswich. He then left for Warwick and built the Warwick Arms Hotel and held the licence from 1856–1858.

November 19 (Yates) Jubb's bank entries indicate the receipt of a dishonoured cheque from a person named Yates (£9/16/6). Within a few weeks this was replaced with a valid cheque. Several persons named Yates were located in the Ipswich area in the mid-1850s but with no supportive links as to why they would be doing business with Jubb. A report in the *Queensland Times* in 1912 mentioned a carrier called William Yates who operated between Ipswich and Drayton in the mid-1850s but was killed in a carrier accident and the work was taken over by his son John. This Yates is a possibility. Yates was operating from Ipswich and given Jubb's isolated location he would have periodically needed the assistance of carriers.

1857

July 29 (Berkmann) Marcus Berkman from a Germanic and Jewish background was a convict who worked for Fred Bracker, the then manager of Rosenthal Station, which was owned by the Aberdeen Co. Bergman purchased an allotment in Warwick and constructed the first brick general store there. This store was highly successful and Berkman reinforced this income flow from other sources. In 1850 with Hugh Shanklin as a partner they obtained registration to operate as Spirit Merchants. Berkman also purchased alluvial gold when it was available.

The 'warring' innkeepers Jubb and Fleming both had bank entries relating to business with Berkman. Jubb made a comparatively small expenditure to Berkman of £3. Patrick Fleming had apparently borrowed money as his remaining bank entries indicate he repaid Berkman £210/1/10 on 19 January 1858. This bank entry actually states 'Paid Berkmann int' and this has several possible interpretations. The positive interpretation of this is that £10/1/10 was interest and £200 capital repayment. Two days later Fleming paid Berkman another £200. Bergman continued to do business with Fleming as he paid him £99/18/10 on 25 February 1858. Berkman and Fleming knew each other well. Berkman's first marriage was to Fleming's sister Bridget. This marriage ended tragically with Bridget's death in 1857. The first land sale occurred in Warwick in 1850 and Fleming and Berkman both purchased £8 half acre allotments.

Fleming had also borrowed £100 from Christopher Gorry, the saddler, and this was repaid on 5 September 1857.

It seems highly likely that the borrowing by Fleming was linked to the ownership of some asset or the development of a business opportunity. The *Warwick Daily News* reports that Fleming built the Downs Inn and the *NSW Archives* indicate that in 1853 Fleming held the licence for the Inn. However, the *Empire* reported in January 1854 that Mort and Co had sold the Downs Inn for £800. Fleming took up the licence for the Rising Sun Inn at Millfied near Cessnock and over the next few years the licence for the Downs Inn was held by John Bellamy, Robert Dix and Thomas Gray. Fleming again held the licence for the Downs Inn in 1858. It seems possible that the repayment of £500 plus interest to Berkman and Gorry between September 1857 and January 1858 meant he was now the owner again as well as the licensee of the Downs Inn.

The financial arrangement between Gorry, Berkman and Fleming occurred at a time when Berkman was identified as a wealthy man. Ward-Brown in her *Rosenthal* chapter on the history of early Warwick described how the finances of the early Warwick businesses must have been 'very enmeshed' and they folded like 'a pack of cards' in a period of financial difficulty in 1860. Among those declared bankrupt was Berkman. Two years after Fleming repaid the money to Berkman he was involved in another business transaction relating to Jubb's stock.

October 29 (Wilson & Co) George Harrison Wilson emigrated from Newfoundland and became a successful Ipswich business man with an agency that dealt with wool, land, cattle, sheep, seed potatoes and station employment. In three payments during 1857 and 1858 Jubb paid a total of £33 to Wilson & Co.

November 12 (Balbi) Alexander Balbi was a well-known innkeeper in the Fassifern area who held the licence for the Bush Inn from 1856 to 1858. Later he built the Halfway House Hotel at Clumber. Balbi received £3 from Jubb in November 1857.

1858

March 8 (Macalister) In March 1858 Jubb paid Arthur Macalister £2/2/-. Macalister was a solicitor who owned 68 acres on the Bremer River. He was involved in politics and became Premier of Queensland in 1866.

March 9 (Gray & Co) Walter Gray had worked nine years in an Edinburgh lawyer's office before emigrating to NSW. In 1841 he was appointed the first assignee under the new Insolvency Act. While in Ipswich he was a general and shipping agent and did accountancy work. He was appointed a JP in 1859 and had an early involvement in coal at Tivoli near Ipswich. Jubb paid Gray & Co £4 in 1858.

March 9 (Jones & Co) T H Jones & Co traded as iron mongers in Ipswich and Jubb paid them £1 in 1858.

March 13 (Bailie) James Bailie was proprietor of the Victoria Hotel, Ipswich in 1858 and he was paid £38/10/- by Jubb. A payment of this amount was equivalent to what many labourers in the colony earned in a year. Bailie was a registered Ipswich brewer in the early 1850s and perhaps this business continued and Jubb made some bulk purchases for the Woolpack Inn. Bailie had other strings to his bow and in 1855 he advised his patrons he was moving to new premises and thanked them for supporting his activities as a 'store keeper, engineer, millwright and general merchant'. An interesting man, as from 1856 to 1858, he held a hotel licence.

March 15 (No 29) Paid £5 by Jubb. There was no evidence located as to who was the owner of the account described as No 29.

March 19 (...aley) Paid £1 by Jubb.

Although Jubb used cheques there is little doubt that cash acquired from the activities of the inn were used for some of his expenses. For example, his several donations to McGinty for the construction of churches in Ipswich and Warwick do not appear in his bank account. It is highly likely that Jubb's most expensive purchases related to the supplies that arrived from Sydney. This expenditure is not recorded in the bank entries of 1856 to 1858. Looking at the firms Jubb dealt with, the broad based agency of Wilson & Co was perhaps the type of company that may have arranged Jubb's imports from Sydney.

The withdrawal of £150 by Jubb on 16 January 1857 raises an interesting possibility. Several weeks after this withdrawal Jubb took a steamer to Sydney and then out to Parramatta where at the Rose and Crown public house the 'shambles at Parramatta' began. Was this withdrawal associated with the £5 notes evidenced in the incident at Parramatta?

George Jubb

There is little doubt that George Jubb had a serious drinking problem. It is distinctly possibility that William may have had a drink or two before contacting the *Moreton Bay* Courier in 1860 and it appeared that his life was on a similar trajectory to that of his brother.

In 1859 George was no longer working at Woolpack Inn. The *Moreton Bay Courier* in June 1859 stated George was camped on Warwick Range with George Taylor where they were working with a bullock team. This is not a drinking incident but it demonstrated George's capacity to get into trouble. George was actually employed as a cook. Taylor told George to go and get water but George decided to take some time to light his pipe. This annoyed Taylor who struck George. Unfortunately George responded by using the knife he had in his hand to stab Taylor in the back. Dr Samuel Aldred said the wound was not dangerous but large and deep. A Supreme Court hearing before Judge Lutwyche sentenced George to six months hard labour.[25] He was discharged from the Brisbane prison 8 December 1859.

Four years later in 1863 the *North Australian and Queensland General Advertiser* reported that George Taylor, the man stabbed by George Jubb, was still working as a bullock driver. He was employed in a team of drivers acting as carriers between Ipswich and Warwick. Taylor fell off his wagon on the Warwick Road, was run over and the inquest returned a verdict of accidental death.[26]

In 1871 George was in court at Dalby on a charge of obscene language, and in 1874 the *Queensland Post Office Directory p.192* lists George as a blacksmith at Forest Vale, Queensland. The *Western Star and Roma Advertiser* in 1876 listed the names of all those donating money to the Roma Hospital. George Jubb was named as making a donation of £1/10/- and was identified as being at Mitchell Downs, a pastoral run four miles out of Mitchell.[27] In other words George remained in the general locality 'out west' but moved around, probably as a consequence of being a mobile blacksmith in an area of scattered low populations.

There was more than one George Jubb living in Queensland during the 1880s. The *Gaol Description and Entrance Book for 1883* names a George Jubb in Darlinghurst Prison for two days in March of 1883: the reason for the imprisonment was drunkenness. It could well be the blacksmith visiting the city. In September of 1886 the *Queensland Police Gazette* reported a robbery had occurred at the house of George Jubb, Mitchell. Three £5 notes and a £1 note were stolen and the suspect was identified as G H Gregory who had been staying at a local hotel but left the day after the money disappeared. A complete description was given of this apparently retired army officer from Scotland who lived on a pension. The police considered this a 'very doubtful report'. It is assumed this referred to the suspect and not the complainant George Jubb. No further information was located regarding the robbery.

No other information could be found about George until 1896 when the *Charleville Times* and other regional newspapers reported his death. It was reported that the old man had lived in the Maranoa for many years. It was at least for 25 years. He had set out to ride from Redford to Forest Vale. These locations were actually pastoral stations and if the 1871 Census is taken as a guide, there were seven houses and 27 inhabitants in Redford and three houses and 33 inhabitants at Forest Vale.[28]

George was described as a blacksmith and wheelwright and was travelling with pack horses. It seems likely that these horses carried his tools of trade as he moved around the isolated stations in the outback. He wandered off the track 15 miles from Redford in cold and wet weather. His body was later found by a blacktracker. George was described as an 'old' man of 'infirm' health and partially 'blind'.

The *Western Star and Roma Advertiser* carried a very similar account of George's death. The exception was that a member of that paper's staff knew about the Woolpack Inn and how both Jubbs had been there and ran a blacksmith and wheelwright shop as well as the inn. There was also a comment that it would have been a better outcome if George had been convinced to go to an institution such as that at Dunwich where he could obtain care. This reference was to the Dunwich Benevolent Asylum.

In 1887 the *Western Star and Roma Advertiser* carried a notice indicating that George Jubb of Mitchell had died without making a will and that there would be an auction at the Mitchell court house of the following items: a saddle, a tomahawk, a razor and some other unlisted items. We come into this world with little and we can depart with very close to the same.[29]

Shipping Intelligence

Jubb was running the Woolpack Inn from 1850 to 1859 and as it provided accommodation, food and alcohol, the obtaining of supplies was a major issue. We know that Jubb visited Warwick, Stanthorpe and Ipswich, but these were relatively small villages at the time. He also made trips to Brisbane and Sydney, but there is no mention of obtaining supplies on such trips. The 'Shipping Intelligence' column of the *Moreton Bay Courier* does provide some details of the supplies carried by coastal steamers from Sydney to Brisbane for Jubb. Some of the steamers involved were the *Boomerang, Tamar, Bella Vista* and *Yarra Yarra*.

Some years Jubb received goods from Sydney more than once a year and other years no records of goods arriving were located.

Most of the supplies recorded are what would have been necessary purchases for an 1850's inn. However, there are several items that warrant comment. Certainly 1856 appears to have been a good year, not only is this based on the 6 hogsheads received, but on the purchasing of 12 grindstones for use by a blacksmith. The 16 drums

William Jubb: From Promise to Disaster

of nails, lead and stoves suggests that Jubb was, to some extent, still associated with the building trade.

Year	Imports For Jubb
1851	1 case, 1 cask, 1 hogshead of brandy, 1 bag of salt and 1½ chests of tea.
1852	1 bag of salt, 4 cases of gin, 3 dozen of brandy, 4 bags of sugar, 1 keg of peppermint, 1 hogshead of rum and 1 quart cask of brandy
1854	11 dozen, 23 dozen and 2 dozen.
1856	20 dozen, 6 hogsheads, 1 cask, 8 dozen pipes, 1 bundle of pails, 12 grindstones, 40 camp ovens, 2 stoves, 16 drums of nails and 3 pieces of lead.
1857	1 dozen and 10 bags of plums.
1858	1 case of jam, 1 case of pickles, 2 cases of fruit, 1 box of soap and 26 packages.
1859	1 horse.

The 40 camp ovens and 8 dozen pipes may indicate that Jubb anticipated a considerable number of travellers to be passing by the inn looking for equipment to make the most of possible new opportunities.

Jubb purchased 36 dozen bottles of alcohol in 1854. It is assumed that he purchased various types of alcohol and given this quantity there was clearly an expectation of good sales.

The purchasing of a keg of peppermint in 1852 is of interest. This may have been used as a flavouring during cooking or as a medicinal product. Peppermint had long been used for flatulence, stomach pains, diarrhoea, nausea and indigestion. Whether it was effective is another question. It is possible that the keg of peppermint was an important medical standby for the Jubbs. It could also be used to restore or disguise the flavour of meat.

During Jubb's time at the Woolpack he ran stock in the surrounding area and it is likely he did his own butchering or arranged for this to be done on site.

Woolpack Inn Ownership

As interest in the Darling Downs increased, the Woolpack Inn had the opportunity to provide food, alcohol and accommodation to those seeking new opportunities. Many would be riding horses or using drays and wagons. As the Jubb brothers were blacksmiths they probably had many opportunities to demonstrate their skill. It is highly likely that Jubb made a good living at the inn. He could afford a private cabin when travelled by steamer to Sydney and on two occasions was reported as carrying in excess of £100 at inns.

Jubb moved to the Woolpack Inn at the right time and as the reports spread regarding the immense potential of the Darling Downs, Jubb was on the verge of a promising financial future. Despite this, Jubb's life on the Darling Downs was somewhat unsettled and much of this can be linked to his own behaviour, especially when he was away from the Woolpack Inn.

His first wife, Margaret, died in an accident and the drinking by his brother, George, was a recurring problem. There were the court cases that must have disrupted his business life. He was robbed in Parramatta, his wallet was probably stolen in Ipswich, his horses were stolen and his servant claimed Jubb had threatened to shoot him. Another publican took him to court over signatures on cheques. He was imprisoned illegally and formally warned others about illegally selling his stock or property without his permission. These issues disrupted the life of this Irish innkeeper, but his disagreement with Arnold Wienholt was the most concerning as his very livelihood was challenged.

It is possible that the dispute with Wienholt may have begun before the argument about a debt and an eventual court case in 1851. The magistrates ruled that Wienholt owed a debt of £9/19/- to Jubb. Wienholt unsuccessfully appealed this decision in the Supreme Court. The outcome of the case certainly would not have helped their relationship. This dispute continued until June 1859.

The complexity of the details of the dispute between Jubb and Wienholt is presented in detail by James Gill in *Spicer's Peak Road*. This book presents only an overview of the complex events that occurred.

In summary, the Woolpack Inn was built on Glengallan Run with the permission of Colin Campbell. This section of land was soon transferred to a run held by Wienholt, and from this time onwards the ownership of the buildings constituting Woolpack Inn was questioned. Wienholt wrote of his pre-emptive rights and Jubb was concerned about the capital he had invested in the area and the years spent building up a business. Letters, petitions and requests were sent to many people by Jubb and Wienholt. Probably the only period of time when silence prevailed was when Arnold Wienholt was in United Kingdom from late 1855 to mid-1857. Various communications relating to the Woolpack Inn were made with significant people. These included Colonel George Barney, Lt Governor of Northern Australia, Stephen Simpson, Commissioner of Crown Lands, Christopher Rolleston, Commissioner of Crown Lands and then Registrar General, Arthur Wood, Assistant Surveyor, the Secretary for Lands and Public Works, Major Thomas Mitchell, Surveyor General, Augustus Gregory, Sir Charles Fitzroy the Governor General.

The final decision was in many ways a compromise. The pre-emptive right of Wienholt was recognised but a compassionate decision was afforded to Jubb as he was placed under the protection of 1851 regulations. This meant the land in dispute would go to auction with one lot being a 22 acre fenced area which contained the inn and other buildings. These improvements were valued at £850. In June of 1859 the lot was auctioned at Warwick.[30]

Wienholt obtained the lot on which the inn stood. Jubb did not enter a bid. Perhaps he did not have enough money to make a competitive bid against a man with Wienholt's resources. Alternatively it is possible that by then Jubb had lived a tough life and was a disillusioned and worn down innkeeper. Bartley, in his book wrote that in July 1859 he found 'the old man pulling down the ancient hotel, where so many of the olden stories had passed, and bygone yarns were spun'.

Jubb may have looked old, but assuming his birth was in 1813, he was actually only 46 year old. When Jubb applied for the land surrounding the Woolpack Inn the surveyor, Arthur F Wood, drew a survey plan. In April 1858 this survey was forwarded to the Surveyor General. Written on the face of this survey was the following; '60 days to be allowed for the removal of improvements should Jubb not become the purchaser'.

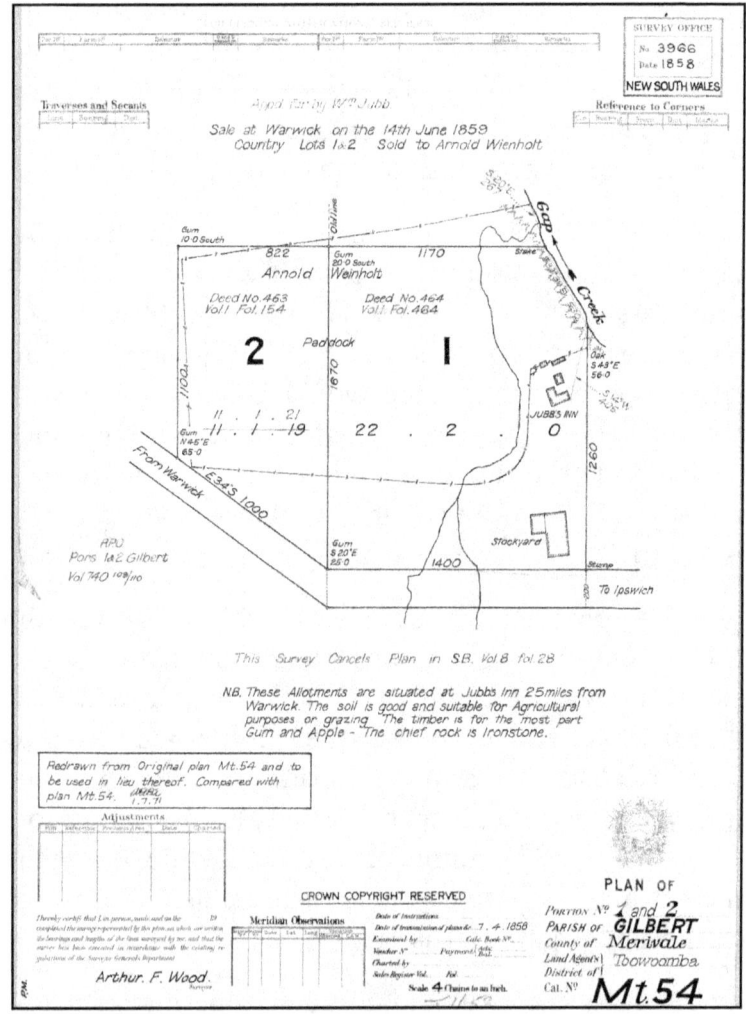

7. Map of the Woolpack Inn Sale Site. (1859).

Jubb wrote to the government in July 1860 asking if they had any objection to him selling the timber from his Cunningham Gap house. This was agreed to. The letter to the government requested replies should go to W Jubb at Mr Paynter's, Nicholas Street, Ipswich. This may well have been Mr Thomas Paynter who was secretary and librarian at the Ipswich School of Arts but soon after moved to live out of town. Jubb then placed an advertisement in the *North Australian, Ipswich and General Advertiser* indicating that he had for sale about 3000 feet of house timber and a quantity of cedar doors and sashes.[31]

When Jubb wrote to the government he had decided that he would be 'going to the interior as soon as possible'. This was probably a throw-away line, but who knows, a man like Jubb may have been thinking of another location for an inn. This looked like an end for Jubb in the Darling Downs and the new colony of Queensland. This was far from the reality.

Cattle Stealing

The first we hear about the possibility of Jubb's stock being stolen and sold comes in January of 1859 when Jubb placed a notice of caution in the *Moreton Bay Courier*. Actually, the notice is more complex than the possibility of missing stock. Jubb's caution expresses his concern that people were selling his cattle and other property without his permission and that the stock were branded with WJ.[32]

He also warned against giving credit to people in his name. Legal action was threatened against those involved in such activities. No precise details could be located about the activities Jubb alluded to.

A far more serious situation was revealed in the *North Australian, Ipswich and General Advertiser* two years later. By August 1861 Jubb was apparently being accused by his second wife (Eleanor Sherriff) and members of her family of stealing cattle. At this time Jubb was living in Wharf Street, Ipswich. It is impossible to reconstruct what the real story was regarding the alleged stealing of cattle. Jubb's relationship with his wife and her family certainly appeared to have totally broken down and Jubb challenged them about their accusations. He placed the following notice in the *North Australian* newspaper.

Notice

The undersigned hereby gives notice that having been accused by his wife and several members of her family of cattle stealing, he has been living in Ipswich above three months expecting a valid charge to be made against him, what he is prepared to disprove. Any person making such a charge after this time will render himself liable to an action for defamation of character.

William Jubb
Wharf Street[33]

In the same issue of the *North Australian* as above Jubb placed a caution notice that read as follows:

Caution

Storekeepers and the public are hereby cautioned against giving credit to any persons whatever in the name of the undersigned, unless by written order from him.

William Jubb
Wharf Street

The caution notice was obviously intended to ensure that Mrs Jubb or members of her family did not involve Jubb in additional expense. Despite the apparent seriousness of the claims no further newspaper comment was found regarding the possibility that Jubb stole cattle.

In 1861 when there was talk of cattle stealing Jubb was involved in two issues brought before the Small Debts Court. One case was with Michael Sullivan and the court decided it had no jurisdiction in the case and it was dismissed. The other case with Thomas Moloney was settled out of court. In both cases no amounts were mentioned and Jubb was the plaintiff. It is impossible to state whether these claims arose from dealings with the old Woolpack Inn or matters that had occurred after Jubb moved to Ipswich.

The *North Australian, Ipswich and General Advertiser* in November 1861 contained a for sale notice from William Jubb that read as follows:

> A first rate team of WORKING BULLOCKS, 10 in number, with Dray, Bows, Yokes, Chains and new Tarpauling, Axe and Cooking Pots. All complete for the road. For particulars apply to the undersigned at the STEAM PACKET HOTEL, Ipswich.
>
> William Jubb[34]

The offer to sell his bullock team suggests that Jubb had made the decision to bring to an end his association with remote inns and convert his assets to cash. It is possible that Jubb was now living at the Steam Packet Hotel, and if this was the case, it was hardly a sensible choice for a man who seemed to enjoy his drink too much. Alternatively, it may have just been a convenient location to meet potential customers. An interesting aside concerning the Steam Packet Hotel was that by 1863 Henry Alphen held the licence.

The newspaper reports tend to convey Jubb as a man frequently in difficult situation. This would surely not have been the case when Governor Sir Charles Fitzroy was at the Woolpack. In 1854 Fitzroy made a tour of Moreton Bay Region, and his party stayed overnight at both the Bush Inn at Warrill Creek and the Woolpack Inn at Gap Creek. Undoubtedly that 'brawny bit of stuff', William Jubb, and his loquacious wife Margaret would have been on their best behaviour in attending to such a distinguished party of paying guests. It would not be surprising if the Governor departed thinking what wonderful hosts the innkeeper and his wife were.

David Robinson

In September 1862 David Robinson entered the story of William Jubb. Robinson was a bootmaker who lived in North Brisbane. He was Jubb's brother-in-law as Eleanor Sherriff, Jubb's second wife, was his sister. Robinson placed a 'notice to the public' in the *North Australian and Queensland General Advertiser* concerning the horses and cattle belonging to Jubb. He contended that Jubb had given him the legal authority to sell these animals and that this had been done. Patrick Fleming of Warwick had purchased the stock.[35]

This was the same Fleming, a licensee of the Downs Inn, who had been involved in a Supreme Court case with Jubb in 1859. Robinson signed the notice in the paper and it was witnessed by John Oxenham a solicitor from Warwick. In October 1859 Jubb took out a writ against Oxenham claiming £41/11/-. The reason for this claim is not known nor could a legal proceeding be located which provided evidence of an outcome. Given prior litigation, it is doubtful that Jubb would have selected Fleming and Oxenham as the most appropriate persons to be associated with the purchase of his horses and cattle. Robinson seems an odd choice to arrange the stock sale, especially as Jubb lived for another 13 years.

The 'notice to the public' also carried an addendum signed by Fleming cautioning the public about molesting the stock he now legally owned. This 'notice to the public' appeared in the same newspaper six times over the next 12 months.

In November 1864 the *Rockhampton Bulletin and Central Queensland Advertiser* reported that David Robinson who had been working in Rockhampton as a bootmaker for some months had been found dead. He had taken strychnine. The paper's report stated that 'he had been drinking during Sunday, Monday and Tuesday [and was] in very low spirits as a consequence of losing a case at court'. The coroner's report mentioned the effects of drink and depression.[36]

The precise nature of the court case lost by Robinson was not located. However, the *Maryborough Chronicle* does mention Robinson's 'drinking spree' and a case against Mr Feez. The Mr Feez mentioned was most likely Albrecht Feez who became an alderman and JP in Rockhampton. He certainly was involved in a number of court cases but a case involving Robinson was not located.

> 'It was only on Thursday last that he [Robinson] was sufficiently sober to appear in the police court to give evidence in a claim he had preferred against Mr Feez'.[37]

Similarly there is no information as to whether Robinson's wife and three children were living in Rockhampton.

It is quite challenging to accept a chain of events revealed in newspaper reports represents the reality of what actually occurred in the 1860s regarding Robinson and Jubb and the stock sale. In September 1862 Robinson reported he had legal permission, possibly power of attorney, to sell Jubb's stock to Fleming, a man Jubb had engaged in prior contentious litigation. This sale was followed two years later when, Robinson, working as a bootmaker in Rockhampton, and was described as being depressed and alcoholic, committing suicide.

Where Did William Jubb Go?

From the time Jubb left the Woolpack Inn it became extremely difficult to explain what happened. He moved down to Ipswich. His marital relationship was completely on the rocks. Eleanor, his wife, and members of her family had apparently spread rumours suggesting he had stolen cattle. Jubb's response was anger. A notice was placed in the newspaper challenging relatives to bring charges against him. This did not happen. His brother-in-law, Robinson, apparently obtained permission to sell Jubb's stock. This did not sound like Jubb as he invariably attended to his own business activities. Robinson the bootmaker had moved to Rockhampton and ended his life by taking strychnine.

Why did Jubb give Robinson, an alcoholic, permission to sell his stock? Where was Jubb from 1862 onwards? What were the possibilities? Throughout this innkeeper's story there were indications that he periodically drank to excess. Did he become alcoholically incompetent? Did he move away to the interior as he stated in a letter? Did he have a breakdown?

Many searches were made of the digitised newspapers, and eventually the answer revealed was a sad outcome in the life of William Jubb. The *Brisbane Courier* in January 1865 contained the following note from the Central Police Court, Brisbane.

> LUNACY—William Jubb, brought up on suspicion of being of unsound mind, was remanded for medical testimony.[38]

The turbulence and stress of Jubb's life had simply caught up with him. A partial explanation of what occurred when he left the inn now exists. Sadly, he was simply not coping with life and did not appear to have the capacity to arrange his business or private life. In August 1861 Jubb gave his address as Wharf Street, Ipswich, and by November 1862 he is providing the Steam Packet Hotel as a contact point in Ipswich. By 1865, when he was 52, he appeared before Central Police Court in Brisbane. It is possible that he had moved to Brisbane and that he was being accommodated by a Brisbane relative.

Jubb at Wolston Park

Jubb was admitted to Wolston Park Hospital on the 18 January 1865, and the admission document reported incorrectly that Jubb was 60 years old and described him as a 'bushman and publican'. The age on Jubb's admission documents was probably a guess based on his physical appearance. He was described as suffering from dementia and that this was caused by his 'intemperance and exposure'. The Wolston Park documents contained a note which stated that Jubb had been addicted to drink for many years.

One week after admission on 25 January the Jubb file contained an entry indicating he was 'greatly improved'. He was released from Wolston Park on 6 August 1865; thus spending almost 7 months in care. It should be noted that on the first day of admission to Wolston Park, Jubb was given 'opening medicine'. This may not be the answer for dementia but it may have improved his general well-being. In addition to 'opening medicine' Jubb was given some cough [undecipherable word] work. It would seem that he completed what were probably coughing exercises every day while at Wolston Park.

Letters to the Colonial Secretary in 1868 contain a report of an inquiry into the asylum. Jubb is listed as a patient admitted and discharged in 1865 but his 'native country' is incorrectly stated as England.

When Jubb was released from Wolston Park there is no indication as to where he lived. His son-in-law, James Lloyd, may have looked after him. As the Lloyds had six children it would seem an immense burden to take into the household an ageing man who was an alcoholic and suffering from dementia. Another possibility was that he gained admission to an institution such as Dunwich Benevolent Asylum as a number of their residents had similar physical and social problems to that of William Jubb. The Dunwich records, Government gazettes and Queensland State Archives were searched from 1865 to 1878, and no evidence of Jubb being readmitted to Wolston Park were located.

Unclaimed letters may help in the search for a missing person, and in this case a search of *Queensland Unclaimed Letters Index 1860-74* compiled by the Queensland Family History Society in 2003 provided the following outcomes for versions of the name William Jubb.

1861	Wm Jubb	Brisbane
1862	W Jubb	Ipswich
1863	William Jubb	Toowoomba
1864	W C Jubb	Brisbane
1864	William Jubb	Ipswich
1864	William Jubb	Warwick

1869	Wm C Jubb	Dalby
1872	William Jubb	Rockvale
1873	W Jubb	Dalby

The towns listed above are where the unclaimed letters were received. However, in 1872 (Rockvale) was outside the area Jubb generally lived in and it is approximately 200 kilometres from Mitchell. There was a Rockvale Station and a homestead was built on this station. This station was in a very isolated location and access to alcohol may have been too difficult for the Jubb brothers. In 1864 (Brisbane) and 1869 (Dalby) the initial C was added to the Christian name and the probability of this being William Cephas Jubb becomes rather high. Unclaimed letters were received in 1869 (Dalby) and 1873 (Dalby). As George Jubb made a court appearance in Dalby in 1871 there is a possibility that William had also spent some time in Dalby.

The *Queensland Electoral Roll Indices* were searched for the relevant years but the name William Jubb did not appear. In a number of these years the vote was only given to those who met specific criteria. One such criterion was property ownership and from the time Jubb left the Woolpack he would not have met such requirements.

Jubb's Death

There is a large gap in our knowledge of William Jubb from August of 1865 when he left Wolston Park until his death thirteen years later. The death certificate for William Jubb stated he was a blacksmith who came from Ireland and had lived in the colony for 30 years. He died 24 February 1878 at the age of 65 and was buried in the general section of the North Brisbane Cemetery.

There was no church service for William Jubb as James Lloyd placed a notice in the *Brisbane Courier* inviting his friends to the funeral of William Jubb which would be leaving from his house in Julia Street. Given Jubb's apparent link to the Catholic Church he would not have been impressed that the officiating clergyman was J H Black of the Church of England. Dr John Mullen had seen Jubb a few days before he died and reported that Jubb had died from cancer which he had experienced for some time. Jubb died at Julia Street, Fortitude Valley, where James Lloyd, Jubb's son-in-law lived. Lloyd had married Eleanor's daughter Elizabeth Jane. At the time of Jubb's death his wife Eleanor and son Cephas William (age 20 years) were still alive.

William Jubb: From Promise to Disaster

Cephas William Jubb died at age 27 in 1885. His occupation was given as a saddler and the doctor gave the major cause of death as curves, or some similar word, of the spine and psoas abscess. (An abscess apparently frequently associated with morbidity and mortality). A secondary cause of death was described as exhaustion. His father's occupation was recorded as a wheelwright. The person completing the information on the death certificate was again James Lloyd. However, the Lloyds no longer lived in Fortitude Valley as their new address was 'The Esplanade, Sandgate'. It was noted that this was also the address given for Cephas William Jubb.

Eleanor Jubb

It remains unclear as to what exactly occurred in the relationship between Jubb and his second wife Eleanor. There is no doubt that the marriage became a disaster. Alcohol was a major factor in this disaster. There are two reports that provide information regarding her life with Jubb. The *Queensland Times, Ipswich Herald and General Advertiser* in January 1862 reported that Eleanor charged Jubb with desertion before the Police Magistrate Court. The first hearing was adjourned until the next day as it was suggested the two might come to an agreement. When the case was called the next day neither Eleanor nor William Jubb made an appearance. The case suddenly ended.[39]

The *Courier* in January 1862 reported the steamer *Yarra Yarra* experienced engine failure on the trip from Sydney to Brisbane but disaster had been avoided. The passengers placed a 'thank you' letter in the paper to Captain Bell and among the signatories were Eleanor, her daughter Elizabeth Jubb and Mrs Robinson, Eleanor's mother. At least the grandmother, mother, and daughter seemed to have been on reasonable terms.[40]

It was initially not known where Eleanor lived. It was possible that she was with her daughter, Elizabeth

Lloyd, at Julia Street. However, given the ill feeling between Jubb and his wife Eleanor, it is difficult to believe they lived in the same house in Julia Street. The accommodation problem was solved by Ann Robinson.

Eleanor and her mother, Jane Robinson, were fortunate that Ann Robinson (Eleanor's sister) married into a family in the hotel business, the Chisholm Campbell's. In 1863, Jane Robinson, the mother of Eleanor Jubb and Ann Campbell died at the Prince of Wales Hotel, Brisbane. When Eleanor Jubb died in 1876 she was living at another of the Chisholm Campbell hotels, the Osbourne in Fortitude Valley. In descriptions of the Prince of Wales and Osbourne Hotels it was noted both had private apartments for clients. The *Courier* 18 January 1864 mentioned that the Osbourne was a two story brick building 'situated in the most healthy part of the locality'. It was further stated that every type of accommodation was catered for 'especially for invalids and others requiring the luxury of fresh air'.

There was another link between the Osbourne Hotel, Colin Chisholm Campbell and relatives of William Jubb. In 1883 Colin Chisholm Campbell took ill and experienced trembling and vomiting. He died at Doughboy Creek on 15 November 1883. An inquest was held and excessive drinking and delirium tremors were mentioned. When probate was declared the sole executor was Jubb's son-in-law James Lloyd of Julia Street. There appears to have been only one monetary benefactor from the will and that was James Lloyd who received £500, a large sum of money for that time.

Reflecting on Jubb

There is always some frustration when a writing task cannot be carried to a neat and tidy conclusion. This is certainly the case when considering the life of William Jubb. There are questions surrounding the how, when and why Jubb, and at least his mother, arrived in New South Wales. Then there are the 13 years between his release from Wolston Park Asylum and his death. If his son-in-law and wife (the Lloyds) took him in, there should be a statue erected to them in Julia Street. They had a number of young children and Jubb was a long-time alcoholic with some degree of dementia, eventually suffering from cancer. Frustration, yes it would be satisfying to have all the gaps in Jubb's life explained. This does not result in negative perceptions regarding the worth of following the Jubb paper trail. Much more has been added to our knowledge of William Jubb. The image of Jubb as a rough and tumble, semi-literate Irishman, living in remote areas of Australia has an appeal.

There is no doubt that William and George Jubb spent a number of years on the Darling Downs. A niggling concern relates to their arrival in Australia. Initially the possibility was explored of William being a convict. Approximately 164,000 convicts were transported to Australia. Although it is known that there are errors in the lists, 17 convicts with the surname Jubb are listed, two being named William Jubb. One of the William Jubbs made his home in Van Diemen's Land. The other arrived in NSW in 1828 aboard the convict ship *Bussorah Merchant*. According to the *Sydney Gazette and New South Wales Advertiser* this William Jubb was granted a certificate of freedom in 1834. However, this Jubb was sentenced in York and it has to be questioned whether in the 1840s the Aberdeen Company, with their preference to employ people from Scotland, would employ an Irish ex-convict as a blacksmith. In all the newspaper items relating to William Jubb there is no mention of a convict background. Similar complexities arose when searching for the appropriate George Jubb. In 1822 a free settler by the name of George Jubb received a land grant in NSW but this was on the Yass River at Sutton in the then named Argyle County. In 1826 the *Australian* identified a convict named George Jubb who had been working on the roads out from Sydney and suffered from dysentery. He was found dead one night and a jury looking into his death determined that he 'died by a visitation of God'.

During the writing about Jubb's life there were times when it appeared that he was on a promising path. Initially at Dalrymple Creek and especially at the Woolpack Inn, he had the opportunity to cement his financial future, but there was the perception he was a man frequently on the edge of trouble. There was also a sadness arising from his downward spiral in life seemingly associated with alcohol and inevitably linked to a potential disaster.

If Jubb is to be viewed as representative of the early hospitality industry, it is somewhat concerning and at times alarming. Perhaps the echoes of another sad alcoholic innkeeper, Jacob Goode of Burnett Inn, can be heard. William and George Jubb both suffered the consequence of too close an association with alcohol. Their plight was a common occurrence in the colony. Several literature sources indicate the intake of alcohol peaked in colonial Australia during the 1830s but that this was probably matched during the gold rushes of the 1850s. The explanation of this social problem partially arises from the fact that the majority of the population did not personally select the colonial as their abode. They were dumped here. It was unfamiliar terrain and the climate, vegetation and some of the animals could be viewed as daunting. Their relatives, friends and known surroundings were thousands of kilometres away. It did not help that 20 years after the arrival of the first fleet the so called 'rum rebellion' occurred and for a period of time rum was a major component of the currency system. Many of those existing, rather than living, in the rugged colonial outposts turned to drink in an effort to reduce the environmental and psychological impact of their new abodes.

The newspapers serving the Moreton Bay District and Darling Downs certainly named those who were charged with drunkenness, advertised temperance meetings and published letters from those concerned about, or totally opposed, to the sale of alcohol. Following the reporting of the 1857 Ipswich licensing meeting the *Empire*, a Sydney based paper, was critical of the number of inns gaining licences in the area. It was stated:

Twenty public houses for 2120 inhabitants ... not much chance of teetotalism progressing in that bustling locality.[41]

As small towns began to develop in the Moreton Bay and Darling Downs Districts it was a rather short time before applications were made for liquor licences.

The information gained depicts Jubb as much more than a blacksmith and publican. One historian's suggestion that Jubb could be described as a 'jack of all trades' opened up a more expansive perspective of the man who ran the Woolpack Inn. It was contended that he was the first person to hold a builder's licence in the Warwick area and Rolleston's records suggest he may have had convict carpenters assigned to work for him. There is even the suggestion that Jubb was involved in the construction of the Woolpack Inn. Rolleston recommended persons for building licences, not for a builder's licence. This problem associated with terminology cannot deny specific evidence that Jubb did have some link to buildings and builders.

The extent of this jack of all trades skill was the appearance of his name in the records of the large Maryland Run. This record relates to Jubb obtaining money for corn and onions. However, he did not obtain all the cash proceeds as a portion went to John Collins, a Warwick publican. This apparent debt to Collins is an omen of the problem in Jubb's life. There was also the comment that Jubb had left the Aberdeen Company but depended to some extent on money orders drawn by John Taylor, manager of the Aberdeen Company. This claimed link to Taylor may not be correct as the one occasion when this link was located in Rolleston's records, the Taylor money order was dishonoured. The information initially obtained regarding Jubb gave no indication that he owned a bullock team. It was not until 1861, when he sold his bullock team that this source of income generation emerged. The Woolpack Inn was located in a strategic position as far as access to Spicer and Cunninghams gaps. It seems highly likely that Jubb would have used this location to benefit from carrying produce down to Ipswich and back up to Warwick and Drayton.

For a period of his life Jubb demonstrated the desire and skills to acquire the financial resources to become an extremely successful man. An addiction to drink made such a dream impossible.

The living conditions Jubb experienced were dramatically different from those experienced by people now living in the Moreton Bay and Darling Downs areas. There is little doubt that the personal costs associated with isolation and loneliness can be great. It is possible that living at an inn where people were coming and going may have, to a certain extent, protected Jubb from such influences. However, he lived in areas where keeping in touch with others involved saddling up your horse and riding off. We do not know how good a horseman Jubb was, but he had a horse stolen from the front door of the Woolpack Inn and another one just 'disappeared'. Late in his time at the Woolpack he had a horse 'imported' on the steamer *Boomerang*. He used a horse and dray to take his ill wife down to Ipswich and his last link with horses may have taken place when Robinson sold his cattle and horses to Fleming in 1862. During the 1850s, when Jubb was at the Woolpack Inn, most of his 'neighbours' owned riding horses and depending on their occupation, a number would have owned dray and draft horses for heavier work.

There were many notable figures with whom Jubb was in contact with but there is no convincing way to mount an argument that such people were his associates or friends. Actually, some of the names listed reflect his legal difficulties. He knew Alfred Lutwyche, Nehemiah Bartley, Patrick Leslie, Patrick Fleming, Benjamin Glennie, Arnold Wienholt, John Clune, Patrick O'Sullivan, Henry Alphen, Daniel Foley Roberts, John Douglas, John Taylor, Joseph Gordon and even Governor Fitzroy. He had the money to travel to Sydney in a cabin on a steamer and mix with well-known colonial figures.

The evidence gained from the remaining bank records of Jubb suggest there were prominent business men in Ipswich and Warwick known to Jubb. To suggest these were his friends is simply guessing.

There is little doubt the jovial Irish innkeeper moved among the significant colonial travellers with a glass in his hand and an exaggerated version of his adventures at Dalrymple Creek and Gap Creek. The question we cannot answer is whether such travellers considered Jubb as one of them or as just a bit of a character they occasionally bumped into or heard about.

There is a list of incidents that made Jubb a person warranting study. On religious grounds he had his first wife exhumed and reburied. The first burial site did not have the appropriate consecrated ground. Probably few in the colony owned a stick gun. Jubb did, and his servant said Jubb threatened to shoot him with it. After visiting an Ipswich hotel, his wallet was apparently stolen. A publican took Jubb to court over the signatures on two cheques. Forgery was not the problem. Jubb's defence was that the cheques should not have been accepted as he was in an alcoholic stupor and did not know what he was doing. Following one court case Jubb was given a six months sentence but a higher court reversed the decision stating that it was a case of illegal imprisonment. Jubb, in 1859, complained that others were stealing his stock and property. He also issued a warning about giving credit to people when he had not authorised such actions. By 1861 the boot appeared to be on the other foot and Jubb placed a notice in the newspaper claiming that his wife Eleanor and other relatives of hers were spreading rumours about him stealing cattle. He challenged them to produce evidence of this, but nothing eventuated. His wife Eleanor eventually charged him with desertion. Both arrived for the first day of the hearing but neither returned for the second day of the proceedings. The case just lapsed.

There were six issues which tend to define William Jubb more than all the others. These were what I have called, being a diversified man, being involved in a 'shambles at Parramatta', his brother George, the dispute with Arnold Wienholt, examining the role played by David Robinson, and the charge of lunacy.

Initially no financial records of William Jubb were located. During the period of data collection it is clear that Jubb had the capacity to acquire income from several sources. He was capable of working as a blacksmith and an innkeeper. He had some links to the construction of buildings. He owned a bullock wagon, ran cattle on nearby land and on at least one occasion was involved in the barter trade. It is quite likely that in some years he had a substantial income. He was described by one historian as a 'jack of all trades' and this was despite being semi-literate. He was a diversified man who, like a number of his associates, became addicted to alcohol.

Jubb made a trip to Parramatta and became involved with the male and female riff-raff of the area. The words that describe what took place were 'alcohol', 'probably prostitutes', 'drugged', 'money stolen', 'violent illness', 'arrests' and 'two years hard labour'. Keep in mind that Jubb somehow explained this 'shambles' to his new wife a few weeks later. It is impossible not to wonder just how well Jubb knew Eleanor before this marriage.

George Jubb, like his brother William, was a blacksmith and both became alcoholics. George had three arrests for drunkenness and obscene language. He eventually stabbed a work mate in the back and went to prison for six months with hard labour. Despite his hard drinking, George lived until he was 75 years old. His death was tragic as he wandered off a track on his horse miles out from Mitchell and died a lonely death on a cold and wet night. What is not known is whether the Jubb brothers were closely associated in the latter parts of their lives. When George left the Woolpack Inn, was this the last contact William had with him? In a previous publication, *The Elusive Archibald Young,* it was apparent that many of the people Young moved among in New South Wales and the Moreton Bay District were of Scottish origin. It is not at all clear whether Jubb immersed himself in an Irish culture in the colonies. Unclaimed mail provides some support for the notion that William may have followed George 'out west' to Dalby or beyond.

The elongated battle over the ownership of the Woolpack Inn and the small acreage surrounding Woolpack Inn created immense concern for Jubb. In simple terms, Jubb appeared to run a successful business on land owned by Wienholt. The land owner wanted the land and the inn but was not interested in compensating Jubb. The eventual suggestion was an auction of the area in dispute. Jubb knew he did not have the resources to outbid Wienholt. He did not make a bid and Wienholt took over the site. It is highly likely that by this time Jubb's general health was poor and continued excessive drinking only compounded his problems. William Jubb's days as an innkeeper appeared over and the decline of a once potentially successful man accelerated.

From 1851 to June 1859 Jubb and Wienholt were involved in a rancorous legal battle regarding the ownership of the Woolpack Inn. In June 1859 Wienholt gained control of the land and inn site which ensured Jubb's livelihood, and by July 1860 Jubb had lost the inn and sold the timber from what had once been his home on Gap Creek. David Robinson, Jubb's brother-in-law had gained permission to sell Jubb's stock. Jubb advertised and sold his team of working bullocks in November 1861. By September 1862 Jubb's cattle and horses had been sold to Fleming. As Fleming had taken a successful legal action previously, the stock sale must have added to the displeasure and humiliation felt by Jubb.

By 1865 the police charged Jubb under the lunacy regulations. This does not imply he was a lunatic in the way we now conceptualise the word. He was a long time alcoholic suffering from exposure and some degree of dementia. Sadly, he could not take care of himself and was admitted to Wolston Park Asylum as a shadow of his former self. From the time Jubb entered Wolston he tended to disappear from mention in the newspapers. He developed cancer and, based on unclaimed letters, he may have made contact with his brother George further 'out west'.

To complete this analysis of William Jubb, it should be mentioned that the meaning of the family name Jubb in old French is 'sorry wretch' and in Hebrew can be traced back to 'persecuted one'. Perhaps when the police and staff at Wolston dealt with Jubb they may have thought he was a 'sorry wretch'. From Jubb's point of view, the aggressive and ongoing dispute with Wienholt may well have made him feel he was the 'persecuted one'.

Postscript
Jubbs (Tubbs) Were Farmers

Perhaps a book is never finished. On May 2, 2018 I received the completed index for the book. On the same day I read an article that both changed and clarified my view regarding the Jubbs at Dalrymple Creek (Allora).

The surveyor James Charles Burnett left Sydney in 1848 to carryout survey work on the boundaries of several Darling Downs runs and to prepare plans for the towns of Drayton, Warwick and Dalby. One of his assistant surveyors was Thomas Davis. The recollections of this assistant were compiled by his son, Arthur Hoey Davis, better known as the Australian literary legend, Steele Rudd who wrote such classics as *On Our Selection* featuring 'Dad and Dave'.

The recollections of Thomas Davis provide a description of a settlement on Dalrymple Creek in the following words:

> A farm worked by William and Geo. Tubb was in full swing on Dalrymple Creek in 1850. When I visited the place that year these brothers had about 15 acres of corn growing. It stood in a flat on the town side where the bridge is, and

the house together with a blacksmith shop was situated where stands Gordon's hotel. They found corn raising paid better than the trade and used to cart produce to Drayton and even as far as Ipswich where it brought as much as 15 shillings and £1 per bushel. On the return trip they carried loading for the shopkeepers... therefore, the Tubbs were the first farmers on the Darling Downs and they were the only residents of Allora at that time. Years afterwards I visited the place and found the selection had been abandoned.[42]

This sheds a new perspective on the reason William Jubb purchased plough wings in 1847 and where Jubb obtained corn and onions to sell to the Maryland Run. We can also add farmer to the list of occupations Jubb was engaged in during his eventful life.

William Jubb Timeline

1813	Born in Ireland.
18xx	Arrived in NSW.
1840s	Blacksmith at Goomburra for Aberdeen Company.
1845	Gave evidence concerning Joseph Gordon.
1845	Left Goomburra.
1845	Some of his money orders still signed by John Taylor.
1846	At Allora applied for a building licence from Rolleston.
1847	Blacksmith supplies arrive; plus plough wings.
1848	Rev. Glennie at Jubbs.
1848	Licence for Woolpack Inn granted to James Fortune.

1850	Patrick Leslie mentions Jubbs.
185x	Maryland Run deal but part of payment to John Collins.
1850	At Woolpack Inn obtains liquor licence.
1850	Liqua mentions the Jubbs in a court case.
1851	Court case against Arnold Wienholt.
1854	Margaret Jubb dies in wagon accident.
1854-55	Horses stolen from Woolpack Inn.
1855	Wallet incident at Queens Arms Hotel, Ipswich
1857	Father McGinty thanks Jubb for donations to the church.
1857	Shambles at Rose and Crown Hotel, Parramatta.
1857	Marries Eleanor Sherriff at Windsor.
1858	Servant James Kelly claims Jubb threatened to kill him.
1858	Son born.
1859	Lost court case to Patrick Fleming regarding cheques.
1851-59	Imports alcohol and other supplies from Sydney.

1959	Woolpack Inn site sold to Arnold Wienholt.
1859	Jubb accuses others of stealing his stock.
1861	Family members accuse Jubb of stealing stock.
1861	Living in Ipswich and sells his working bullock team.
1862	Brother-in-law David Robinson sells Jubb's stock.
1862	David Robinson, an alcoholic, moves to Rockhampton.
1864	David Robinson commits suicide.
1865	Lunacy charge also suffering dementia and alcoholism.
1860s	Unclaimed mail suggests possible living locations.
1876	Eleanor Jubb dies at Osbourne Hotel, Brisbane.
1878	William Jubb dies at James Lloyd's house, Fortitude Valley.
1885	Son dies at James Lloyd's house, Sandgate.

Endnotes

1. *Brisbane Courier,* 10 May 1892, p.2.
2. *New South Wales Government Gazette,* 30 May 1845. Issue No 45.
3. *Examiner,* 18 October 1845, p.86.
4. *Australian,* 21 October 1845, p.3.
5. *Toowoomba Chronicle and Darling Downs General Advertiser,* 19 June 1902, p.5.
6. Ward-Brown, J. (1988). *Rosenthal Historic Shire.* Warwick: Rosenthal Shire Council. Much of this book relates to the area Jubb lived in during the 1840s and 1850s. The most pertinent contents regarding Jubb can be found on pp.531-532 and p.120.
7. *Empire,* 28 December 1861, p.7.
8. Ward-Brown, J. (1988). *Rosenthal,* p.120.
9. *Moreton Bay Courier,* 26 January 1850, p.1.
10. Ward-Brown, J. (1988). *Rosenthal,* pp.531-532.

11. *Moreton Bay Courier,* 22 May 1847, p.2.

12. Ward-Brown accessed the Maryland records then held by Mr V. Greenup and these are now held by Mr G. Greenup.

13. *Warwick Daily News,* 16 March 1922, p.2.

14. *Sydney Morning Herald,* 13 December 1851, p.4.

15. *Moreton Bay Courier,* 19 May 1855, p.2.

16. *Ibid.,* 28 April 1855, p.3.

17. *Ibid.,* 28 April 1855, p.3.

18. *Ibid.,* 8 September, p.5.

19. *Sydney Morning Herald,* 23 May 1857, p.6.

20. To view the Rose and Crown Hotel as it is in 2018 go to the following website (www.roseandcrownhotel.com.au)

21. *Moreton Bay Courier,* 30 October 1858, p.2. The precise nature of Jubb's 'stick gun' is not known. It was probably a 'walking cane gun'. Remington developed a walking cane gun that was a walking stick (cane) which had built into it a compartment containing powder, cap and missile.

22. *Ibid.,* 24 November 1858, p.2.

23. *Ibid.,* 2 March 1859, p.3.

24. *Ibid.,* 20 August 1858, p.2.

25. *Ibid.,* 1 June 1859, p.2.

26. *North Australian and Queensland General Advertiser,* 26 June 1863, p.3.

27. *Western Star and Roma Advertiser,* 8 February 1876, p.4.

28. *Charleville Times,* 25 July 1896, p.2.

29. *Western Star and Roma Advertiser,* 31 March 1897, p.3.

30. The text contains a map providing details of sale of land surrounding the Woolpack Inn.

31. *North Australian, Ipswich and General Advertiser,* 13 July 1860, p.1.

32. *Moreton Bay Courier,* 26 January 1859, p.3.

33. *North Australian, Ipswich and General Advertiser,* 9 August 1861, p.2.

34. *Ibid.,* 15 November 1861, p.2.

35. *North Australian and Queensland General Advertiser,* 13 September 1862, p.4.

36. *Rockhampton Bulletin and Central Queensland Advertiser,* 8 November, 1864, p.2.

37. *Maryvale Chronicle, Wide Bay and Burnett Advertiser,* 19 November *1864.* p.2.

38. *Brisbane Courier,* 14 January 1865, p.5.

39. *Queensland Times, Ipswich Herald and General Advertiser,* 17 January 1862, p.3.

40. Examples of people Jubb travelled with on the steamer were Ratcliffe Pring, who became a member of parliament and QC and William Butler Tooth, a successful pastoralist.

41. *Empire,* 4 May 1857, p.3.

42. S Rudd, (1902). *Recollections of Thomas Davis.* UQ eSpace, Brisbane. Unnumbered 19 page manuscript. Quote from page 4. These *Recollections* were compiled by Steele Rudd and a footnote on p.1 of the document records a compiling date of 1902. It also notes that the document was in the possession of a prominent Queensland politician Hon. Joshua Bell circ. 1908-9. (Jubb being incorrectly named Tubb was the same error made by Lord Montagu when he painted the Woolpack Inn (1853) and used the name Tubb's Inn.)

Sources

BOOKS

Bartley, N. (1892), *Opals and Agates: Or Scenes under the Southern Cross*. Brisbane: Gordon and Gotch.

Connors, L. (2015), *Warrior: A Legendary Leader's Dramatic Life and Violent Death on the Colonial Frontier*. Crows Nest: Allen & Unwin.

Glennie, B. (1848-1860), Typed Manuscript of the *Australian Diary of the Rev. Benjamin Glennie. January 18th 1848 to September 30th 1860*. Queensland State Library. (This is a copy of the document held at St Matthews Church Drayton.)

Grimes, J.A. (2013), *Jacob Goode and his Burnett Inn*. Bloomington: Xlibris.

French, M. (1992), *Pubs, Ploughs & Peculiar People: Towns, Farms and Social Life*. Toowoomba: USQ Press.

Gill, J.C.H. (1981), *Spicers Creek Road: A New Way to the Downs*. Brisbane: Library Board of Queensland.

Hall, T. (1925), *The Early History of Warwick District and the Pioneers of the Darling Downs.* Toowoomba: Robertson & Proven Ltd.

Hansford, B. (2016), *The Elusive Archibald Young: Tracing His Footprints in the Moreton Bay District.* Salisbury: Boolarong Press.

Slocomb, M. (2014), *Among Australian Pioneers: Chinese Indentured Pastoral Workers of the Northern Frontiers 1846-1880.* Bloomingdale: Balboa Press.

Ward-Brown, J. (1988), *Rosenthal-Historic Shire.* Warwick: Rosenthal Shire Council.

DVD

Toowoomba & Darling Downs Family History Society Inc. (2008). *Initial Settlement on the Darling Downs 1843-1852. A transcription of Rolleston's Records.*

LETTER INDEX

Queensland Family History Society (2003). *Queensland Letters Index 1860-74.*

NEWSPAPERS

Allora Advertiser

Brisbane Courier

Courier Mail

Charleville Times

Dalby Herald and Western Queensland Advertiser

Darling Downs Gazette and General Advertiser

Empire

Illustrated Sydney News

Ipswich Herald

Maitland Mercury

Moreton Bay Courier

Northern Australian, Ipswich and General Advertiser

North Australian and Queensland General Advertiser

North Australian

Queenslander

Queensland Times

Queensland Times, Ipswich Herald and General Advertiser

Rockhampton Bulletin and Central Queensland Advertiser

Sydney Morning Herald

Toowoomba Chronicle and Darling Downs General Advertiser

Western Star and Roma Advertiser

Warwick Daily News

Warwick Examiner and Times

Index of People

Aldred, Samuel, 78
Alford, Thomas, 10, 16, 18
Alphen, Henry, 18, 23, 30, 33-4, 38, 53, 61, 92, 111
Anderson, Edward, 12-3
Bailie, James, 71, 76
Balbi, Alexander, 71, 75
Barney, George, 53, 57
Bartley, Nehemiah, 42, 44, 68, 87, 111
Bellamy, John, 74
Berkman, Marcus, 70, 75
Black, J H, 102
Bleaker, Jacob, 12
Bolton, James, 13
Bracker, Fred, 44, 73
Bracker, Harry, 44-5
Burnett, James Charles, 116
Campbell, Colin, 86
Campbell, Colin Chisholm, 105
Challinor, Henry, 48-9
Clune, John, 49, 111
Collins, Catherine, 31
Collins, John, 23, 30-2, 109,
Crabb, William, 4
Cribb, Benjamin, 71-2
Cumming, Frederick, 48

Dalyrmple, Ernest, 14, 20
Davis, Arthur Hoey, 117
Davis, Thomas, 117
Dickinson, John, 46
Dix, Robert, 74
Douglas, John, 62-3, 111
Ferris, Henry, 16
Feez, Albrecht, 95
Flanagan, Peter, 18
Fitzroy, Charles, 87, 93, 111
Fleming, Patrick, 65, 74, 94, 111
Flood, John, 62
Foote, John, 72
Fortune, James, 33-4
Gates, Thomas, 18
Gilbert, 4
Gill, James, 86
Gill, Richard, 71-72
Glennie, Benjamin, 22-3, 25, 111
Goode, Jacob, 5, 108
Gordon, Joseph, 9-10, 111
Gordon, Samuel, 12
Goody, James, 55-6
Gorry, Christopher, 71-2, 74-5
Gray, Thomas, 74
Gray, Walter, 76
Green, Robert, 57
Gregory, Augustus, 87
Gregory, G H, 79
Hack, Mrs, 55
Haigh, Ellen, 55
Haigh, John, 55, 56
Handcock, William, 18
Hold, 4

Horton, James, 13
Horton, William, 18
Hunter & Co, 71-2
Hudson, Frederick, 72
Jones, T H & Co, 71, 76
Jubb, Cephas, 102-3
Jubb, Margaret, 40-3, 48-50, 58, 85, 93
Kelly, James, 60, 62
Laidler, John, 49
Leslie, Patrick, 12-3, 20, 24-5, 33, 38-9, 111
Liqua, 36
Lloyd, James, 100, 102-3, 106
Lutwyche, Alfred, 65, 67, 78, 111
Macalister, Arthur, 71, 75
Marsh, Matthew Henry, 30
McDonald, James, 52
McGinty, William, 50, 76
McEvoy Thomas, 62
Meara, William, 61
Mehan, Stephen, 18
Mercer, Mrs, 49
Miles, Charles, 18
Milford, Samuel, 62
Mitchell, Thomas, 87
Moloney, Thomas, 92
Montagu, Henry, ix, x, 42-3
Mort and Co, 20-1, 23, 74
O'Rourke, Godfrey, 65, 67
O'Sullivan, Patrick, 49, 111
Oxenham, John, 94
Paynter, Thomas, 89
Perryman, John, 23
Platt & Co, 71
Pratten, George, ix, x, 26-7

Pugh, Theophiles Parsons, 68
Reynolds, Margaret, 55
Reynolds, Joseph, 55-6
Ridley, William, 45
Roberts, Daniel Foley, 62, 111
Robinson, Ann, 105
Robinson, David, 114, 94-7, 110, 112, 114
Robinson, Eleanor, 59, 97, 102, 104-5, 112-3
Robinson, Jane, 104-5
Rolleston, Christopher, vii, 9-10, 13-4, 16-9, 26, 38, 87, 109-10
Ross, Neil, 12
Rudd, Steele, 117
Sedolla, Joseph, 4
Schomberg-Kerr, Henry, 43
Shanklin, Hugh, 73
Shea, Timothy, 4
Sherriff, Eleanor, 40, 59, 90, 94
Sherriff, Elizabeth, 59, 102, 104
Sherriff, Richard, 59
Stobart, Henry, 42
Sullivan, Michael, 92
Taylor, George, 78-9
Taylor, John, 14, 17, 21, 109-11
Thorn, George, 51
Therry, Roger, 46
Vowles, William, 70-2
Wienholt, Arnold, 46-7, 53, 86-7, 111-2, 114-5
Wienholt, Edward, 36
Wilks, Henry, 18
Wilson & Co, 71, 75, 77
Wood, Arthur, 87-8
Yates, John, 70-1, 73

www.ingramcontent.com/pod-product-compliance
Lightning Source LLC
Chambersburg PA
CBHW072048290426
44110CB00014B/1597